P9-BZN-280

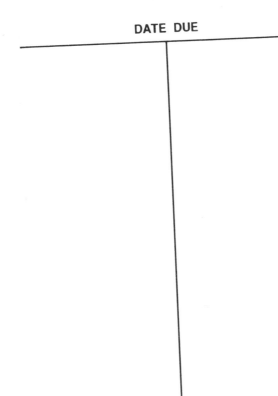

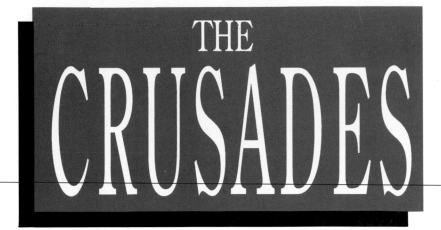

THE CRUSADES

John Child
Nigel Kelly
Martyn Whittock

PETER BEDRICK BOOKS
2112 Broadway
New York, N.Y. 10023

Published by
PETER BEDRICK BOOKS
2112 Broadway
New York, NY 10023

Published by agreement with Heinemann Publishers
(Oxford) Ltd.

Library of Congress Cataloging-in-Publication Data

Child, John, 1951–
    The Crusades / John Child, Nigel Kelly, Martyn Whittock.
    p. cm. – (Biographical history)
    Includes bibliographical references and index.
    ISBN 0-87226-119-0
    1. Crusades – Juvenile literature. I. Kelly, Nigel.
    II. Whittock, Martyn J. III. Title. IV. Series.
    D157.C45 1996
    909.07 – dc20   95 – 44426 CIP AC

Designed by Ron Kamen, Green Door Design Ltd, Basingstoke
Illustrated by Jeff Edwards and Douglas Hall

First American edition 1996
00 99 98 97 96 5 4 3 2 1
Printed in China

The cover shows "Departure for the Crusades", from a
14th century French manuscript.

Acknowledgements

The authors and publisher would like to thank the following
for permission to reproduce photographs:

J. Allen Cash: 1.1A
Aerofilms: 3.2E
Ancient Art & Architecture Collection: 1.3B
Arxiu Mas: 2.5D, 4.4D, 5.2D
Barnaby's Picture Library: 5.6A
Bibliothèque Nationale: Cover, 2.3B, 3.5D
Bibliothèque Royale Albert 1er, Brussels: 4.1D
Bodleian Library, Oxford: 3.6B
Bridgeman Art Library: 2.2A
British Library: 2.3C, 3.1A, 3.3D, 3.4A, 3.8A, 3.8D, 3.9B,
4.3B, 5.1C, 5.1F

British Museum: 4.2C
Chester Beatty Library, Dublin: 1.3D
Corpus Christi College: 3.2A
C. M. Dixon: 1.3C
Edimedia: 1.1C, 2.4D
Frank Spooner Pictures: 5.6B
Giraudon/British Museum: 3.3A
Michael Holford/British Library: 4.4A
Hulton Picture Company: 3.3B
Sonia Halliday Photographs: 1.2A, 2.1A, 2.4A, 3.4E, 3.7A,
3.7F

We would also like to thank the following for permission to
adapt copyright material:

Cadw: Welsh Historic Monuments, Crown Copyright for
Source 5.3A

Every effort has been made to contact copyright holders of
material published in this book. Any omissions will be
rectified in subsequent printings if notice is given to the
publisher.

Details of written sources

In some sources the wording or sentence structure has been
simplified to ensure that the source is accessible.
G. Evans, *Pilgrimages and Crusades*, Chambers, 1976: 3.3G,
3.7B
E. Hallam (Ed.), *Chronicles of the Crusades*, Weidenfeld and
Nicolson, 1989: 2.1B, 2.1C, 2.2B, 2.3A, 2.4C, 2.4E, 2.5A,
2.5B, 2.5C, 3.1B, 3.2C, 3.3C, 3.3E, 3.4B, 3.4D, 3.5B, 3.5C,
3.6C, 3.7C, 3.7D, 4.3A, 4.3C
History Today, March 1987: 3.2B
Hodges and Whitehouse, *Mohammad, Charlemagne and the
Origins of Europe*, Duckworth, 1983: 1.3A
T. John, *The Crusades*, Ginn, 1972: 3.1C, 3.1D, 3.1E, 3.2D,
3.4C, 3.5E, 3.6A, 3.6D, 3.7E, 3.8B, 3.8C, 3.8E, 3.9C, 3.9D,
5.2C, 5.4E
J. Kerr, *The Crusades*, Wheaton, 1966: 3.9A, 5.4B
W. McNeill, *A World History*, OUP, 1979: 5.5D
Medieval World, July/August 1991: 5.1A, 5.1D, 5.1E, 5.1G
R. Moore, *Newnes Historical Atlas*, Newnes, 1983: 5.4C
Z. Oldenbourg, *The Crusades*, Gollancz, 1966: 2.2C, 2.4B, 3.3F
J. Riley-Smith (Ed.), *Atlas of the Crusades*, Times Books, 1991:
4.2D, 5.1B, 5.5A, 5.6C
J. Roberts, *History of the World*, Pelican, 1980: 4.2B, 5.2A,
5.5B, 5.5C
Steven Runciman, *A History of the Crusades*, CUP, 1951: 1.1B,
1.2C, 5.2B, 5.3C, 5.4D
H. Treece, *Know about the Crusades*, Souvenir, 1963: 2.3D
S. Turnbull, *The Book of the Medieval Knight*, 1985: 4.1B, 4.2E
T. Wise, *The Wars of the Crusades*, Osprey, 1978: 4.4E

CONTENTS

1.1 The Fall of Jerusalem

Jerusalem is the place where Jesus was crucified. His body was placed in a tomb there. On the site of this tomb, Christians built the **Church of the Holy Sepulchre**. For Christians, past and present, Jerusalem is the most holy of all cities.

In AD 637 a massive army surrounded Jerusalem. The city had new fortifications and its people held out for almost a year. They hoped a Christian army would be sent to save them. But in February 638, **Sophronius**, the Christian bishop of Jerusalem, was forced to surrender his city. The gates were opened and the enemy entered.

The people of the attacking army were **Arabs**. They were not Christians. They were **Muslims**, members of a religion called **Islam**. Their leader, **Caliph Umar**, rode into the city on a white camel. He was a giant of a man, but very gentle and religious. He had the title 'Commander of the Faithful'. He wore rough and simple clothes. But the army which followed him, mostly Arab tribesmen on horseback, was perfectly disciplined. There was no killing or stealing.

Extract from 'A History of the Crusades' by Steven Runciman, 1951.

The Church of the Holy Sepulchre in Jerusalem.

A SOURCE

A European artist drew this picture of Jerusalem in the Middle Ages. He may never have actually visited Jerusalem, but this picture shows us what he thought about it. The domes and tall towers (minarets) are typical of Muslim mosques.

Umar was taken to the Church of the Holy Sepulchre. When it was time for the Muslims to pray, he left this church and took his prayer mat to another spot. He did not want his followers to turn the church into a Muslim mosque.

Jerusalem was also sacred to the Muslims. They believed that **Muhammad**, the founder of Islam, visited Heaven from Jerusalem. The Muslims built many mosques there. The most famous one is the **Dome of the Rock** (see page 12).

So the Church of the Holy Sepulchre survived and Jerusalem remained the most sacred Christian city. Christians continued to live there. But it was also a sacred city for Muslims and they now ruled it. In time, this led to conflict.

Jesus of Nazareth

Jesus of Nazareth (4 BC–AD 27) was born a Jew in Palestine. At the age of 30 he began to preach a new religion, which became known as Christianity. Over the next three years many people became Christians, and prayed to Jesus as the son of God. The Roman rulers of Palestine disliked the teachings of Jesus. They crucified him. After his death, Christianity spread. By the Middle Ages most of Europe was Christian.

1.2 Islam – Origins and Beliefs

In 570 an Arab called **Muhammad** was born in **Mecca** in Arabia. Followers of Muhammad believe that, at the age of 40, he began to receive messages from God. These messages were the rules for a new religion. Muhammad told his friends; soon many Arabs became God's followers. They called themselves **Muslims** and their religion **Islam**. Muslims believed that Muhammad was God's most important prophet. They recognized Jesus as God's second most important prophet, but not his son.

The key beliefs of Muslims were the '**Five Pillars**'. They were faith, prayer, charity, fasting and pilgrimage. These beliefs remain unchanged to this day.

The first pillar was **faith in God** (**Allah** in Arabic). There was only one God; he made the world and he sent people to Heaven or Hell when they died. The second pillar was **prayer** five times a day. Muslims could pray anywhere, but the prayers had to be said facing in the direction of Mecca. The other three 'pillars' were that all Muslims should give part of their income to **charity** every year; that they should **fast** (go without food) during the Muslim month of **Ramadan**; and promise to go on a **pilgrimage** to Mecca at least once. Muslims based their laws on the **Koran** (Muhammad's messages from God) and **Hadith** (the wise sayings of Muhammad himself). Islamic laws forbade Muslims to eat pork, drink alcohol, gamble or lend money for interest.

Early Muslims in a mosque in Basra.

At first, Muslims had to fight other Arab groups to survive. A war to defend Islam was called a **jihad**. Muhammad said that Muslims who died defending Islam would go straight to Heaven.

By the time Muhammad died in 632, Islam had spread through the whole of Arabia. Then the Arabs expanded into other countries. By 640 they had captured Palestine (including Jerusalem), Syria and Persia; by 710 they had captured the whole of north Africa; by 750 they controlled the whole of central Asia as far as the borders of India and China.

Muslims and Christians

Muslims treated Christians well. They regarded the Christians as misguided in their choice of religion. They encouraged them to convert to Islam; if they did, they were called **mawali** or 'brothers' of the Arabs. But no one was forced to convert. If the Christians refused, the Muslims called them **djimmis** or 'protected people'.

Djimmis had to pay an extra tax, the **jizya**. They also had to obey extra rules. They were not allowed to marry Muslims, or to own arms or horses. But they could keep their churches. Christian pilgrims from other countries were allowed to visit Christian holy places in Muslim countries.

Many of the conquered Christians preferred the Muslims to their old rulers. Earlier rulers had ruled them unfairly, charged them much higher taxes or tried to interfere in their religious beliefs.

Muhammad

Muhammad (570–632) was the Arab founder of the Islamic religion. His followers are called Muslims. The rulers of Mecca, where he lived, did not trust Muhammad or his teachings. He had to move, to Medina, where people accepted his Muslim beliefs.

Medina became a small Muslim state with Muhammad as its leader. The Muslims had to fight to defend their religion. There were many fierce and bloody battles. Muhammad fought in some of these battles. The Muslims were good soldiers, so Islam spread. By 740, Islam stretched from Spain right across northern Africa to the borders of China.

B SOURCE

- Do not build any new churches or repair old ones
- Do not give shelter to enemies of Muslims
- Do not try to stop anyone becoming a Muslim or seek to convert anyone to your own faith
- Do not wear Muslim clothes; instead, wear something that will mark you out as a non-Muslim, for example a brightly-colored hood
- Do not sell intoxicating drinks
- Do not build houses overlooking Muslim houses
- Do not carry weapons or ride horses with saddles
- Do not sing loudly in church or cry noisily at funerals
- Bury your dead away from Muslim graves
- Anyone who attacks a Muslim will no longer be protected.

Rules for Christians in 7th-century Syria, a Muslim country.

C SOURCE

The hearts of the Christians rejoiced at the domination of the Arabs. May God strengthen it and prosper it!

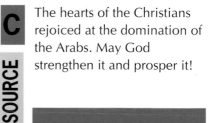

An anonymous Christian chronicler, quoted in 'A History of the Crusades' by Steven Runciman, 1951.

1.3 The Glory of Islam

The Arabs conquered a huge area of land including many famous cities. They collected taxes from all the people they ruled. The Arab rulers, called **caliphs**, became fabulously wealthy.

But the Arabs did not destroy the places they captured. They preserved the cities and the buildings in them. Then they added to them, adapting the styles of buildings they found to create their own distinctive style. Their buildings had many arches, pillars and domes. The Arabs also built new cities, bigger than any before. These had multi-story buildings, sewers and water supplies. They built wonderful palaces and beautiful mosques.

The Arabs conquered some areas where people were skilled at making pottery and glassware. They encouraged local craftsmen to produce artwork the Arabs most liked, especially tilework and miniature paintings. The Arabs also preserved the libraries which they found in conquered cities. They employed scholars to research in them. They built universities, schools and hospitals. The Muslim lands became the most advanced in the world in medicine, astrology, mathematics and geography.

Between about 700 and 1100, the Muslims built the greatest civilization in the world. Europe was backward in comparison.

A **SOURCE**

Their new capital, Samarra, demanded massive spending. The caliph Al-Mutasim built a palace larger than Versailles between 836 and 842. Al-Mutawakkil replaced it with another, almost as large, in about 849–59. Al-Mutamid built his own palace between 878 and 882. The city itself extended along the Tigris for about 35 kilometres (22 miles).

From 'Mohammad, Charlemagne and the Origins of Europe' by Hodges and Whitehouse, 1983. (Versailles is a palace in France built in about 1700. It was built to house the king and his 5,000 courtiers.)

B

The Great Mosque in Damascus, built in 715 by the early Arab caliphs. The arches and pillars are decorated by mosaics, pictures made up of tiny pieces of tiles.

SOURCE

C

SOURCE

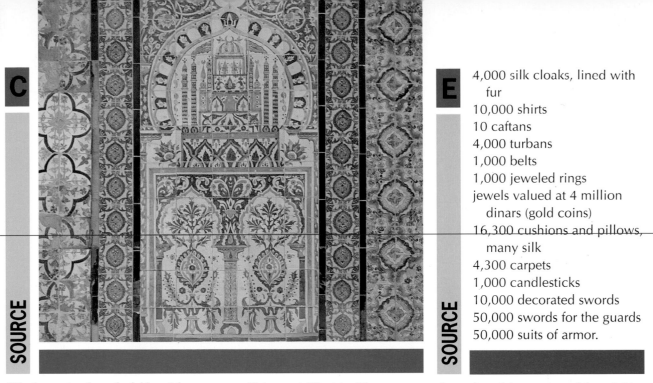

Tile decoration from the lobby of the mosque at Kairouan in Tunisia. The mosque was built in the 7th century.

E

SOURCE

4,000 silk cloaks, lined with fur
10,000 shirts
10 caftans
4,000 turbans
1,000 belts
1,000 jeweled rings
jewels valued at 4 million dinars (gold coins)
16,300 cushions and pillows, many silk
4,300 carpets
1,000 candlesticks
10,000 decorated swords
50,000 swords for the guards
50,000 suits of armor.

Just a few of the contents of the caliph's palace in Baghdad in 809.

D

SOURCE

Harun al-Rashid

Harun al-Rashid (786–809) ruled Islam from his capital of Baghdad. Baghdad was a city of 1.5 million people, five miles across, with schools, hospitals and many public baths. The *Tales of the Arabian Nights* were written about life in Baghdad at this time. They include well-known stories such as those of Alladin and Sinbad. These stories were based on Harun al-Rashid's family.

A miniature painting showing Caliph Mamun (813–33) having a shower, a haircut and a massage in the bath-house of his palace in Baghdad.

1.4 Europe and the Middle East in 1095

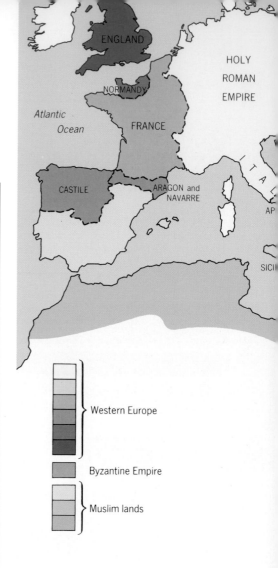

Western Europe was in constant turmoil at this time. Kings fought each other over land; dukes and counts struggled to get land from the kings; heavily armed knights looked for wars where they could earn a living and even win land for themselves. There was a shortage of land and thousands of soldiers available for war.

About the only thing which united the people of western Europe was their Christian faith. Religion was very important to them. The Christians of western Europe were **Catholics** and the Catholic Church had a big influence on their lives. Although Catholics lived in different countries, they all thought of themselves as part of **Christendom**, the Christian community in the world. Christians from all over Europe had joined together on pilgrimages to Jerusalem.

The Holy Roman Empire was a powerful German state which stretched into northern Italy. It was called the Holy Roman Empire because its rulers thought that they were the successors of the original Roman Emperors who used to rule much of Europe. The Holy Roman Emperor was supposed to be the main **defender of the Christian Church** in Europe. But the Pope could not rely on the support of Henry IV, the Holy Roman Emperor at this time, because they had quarreled.

Philip I, **King of France**, had also argued with the Pope. Philip was a weak ruler. He was just powerful enough to rule the area around Paris. But he was constantly struggling to keep control of the rest of France. The Dukes of Lorraine and Aquitaine and the Counts of Flanders, Anjou and Toulouse were the real rulers in their areas. These dukes and counts had their own small armies. But the Duke of Normandy was King Philip's biggest problem.

Normandy was an area of northern France which the French kings had been forced to give to Vikings in 911. The Normans were a warlike people. They produced the most feared mounted knights in Europe. The Norman dukes encouraged these knights to fight abroad so that they did not cause trouble at home.

William the Conqueror died in 1087. The next King of **England**, William Rufus, taxed the English heavily and was worried about leaving England; he feared a rebellion. He was jealous of his brother, Robert, whom William had named Duke of Normandy before he died.

One Norman knight who traveled abroad to find land and wealth was Robert Guiscard. His family captured land in southern **Italy**. His brother, Roger, became Duke of **Sicily**. Robert's son, Robert Borsa, became ruler of Calabria and Apulia. His other son, Bohemund, was also keen to find land to rule.

The Christian kings of Spain were keen to capture nearby Muslim lands. But they were not interested in fighting far from home, and they did not have enough knights to do so.

The Roman Empire collapsed in Europe in about 450. But the eastern half of the Empire survived. Its capital, Constantinople, was built on the site of an old Greek village called Byzantium. Because of this, the Eastern Empire is often called Byzantium or the **Byzantine Empire**. The people there were Christians, but they were not Roman Catholics like the Christians in Europe. They were **Greek Orthodox** Christians. They did not regard the Pope as the leader of their Church. Their Emperor was the head of their country and their religion. The Byzantine Emperor had argued with the Pope about this. The Pope wanted all Christians to think of him as their leader. By 1095 the Byzantine Empire was weak. It had only just survived a long war with the Normans from Italy. The Emperor was also worried about the warlike Turks on his borders.

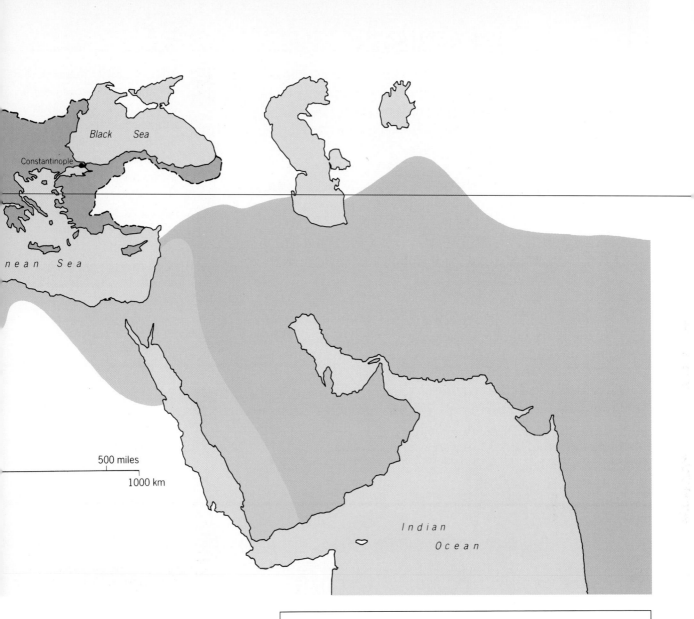

Black Sea

Constantinople

nean Sea

500 miles

1000 km

Indian Ocean

Toghrul-Beg

Toghrul-Beg (1005–63) was the leader of a war-like tribe of Muslim Turks called the Seljuks. In 1055 he brought his army to Baghdad to rescue the caliph from Persian invaders who had taken over Baghdad. In 1056, however, he put the caliph in prison and took over the kingdom himself.

The **Muslim world** was ruled by the Arab caliphs. They were the official successors of Muhammad. The first caliphs were simple and religious men. But later, powerful Arab families used their armies to take over. For a while, the Arab caliphs kept good control from their capital in Baghdad. But later, rival groups took over parts of the Empire. By 1095 the caliph was the official ruler in Baghdad but Muslim power was weakened by the quarrels between the different groups.

The Arab **Fatimid** family in Egypt had taken over real power in the south of the Muslim world.

Further north the **Turks**, a warlike race from central Asia, had invaded Arab lands. They converted to Islam. But their armies bullied the caliphs into doing as they wanted.

The Arabs had conquered most of Spain by 750. But the Christian kings of Navarre, Aragon and Castile were gradually pushing the Muslims back.

2.1 The First Crusade

As you saw on pages 4–5, Jerusalem was a very important city to both Muslims and Christians. Pilgrims from both religions traveled to the city to worship there. The Arab Muslims, who ruled Jerusalem from 638, were quite prepared to let Christians visit the city.

During the 11th century, Muslims from Turkey began to move westwards from central Asia looking for new pastures for their herds. They were a primitive and warlike people who were excellent fighters. They took over Persia, Syria and Egypt. In 1071 the Turks defeated the Eastern Emperor at Manzikert. By 1076 they had captured Jerusalem.

The Turkish Muslims did not agree with Christian pilgrims visiting the **Holy Land** and treated them badly, often robbing and sometimes murdering them. This made Christian people everywhere very angry. The Eastern Emperor, Alexius I, was very worried. The Turks had already begun to capture parts of his Empire. Now they were only 100 miles from his capital in Constantinople. Alexius asked Pope Gregory to help him find forces to fight the Turks. Gregory was unable to help, but the next Pope, **Urban II**, was much keener.

B **SOURCE**

They ruthlessly massacred an immense number of people, carried off a large amount of treasure and took untold numbers of captives, men and women, young boys and girls whom they sold into slavery. So bad was the massacre, that the clear waters of the river suddenly flowed red.

An account of the Turkish attack on the city of Sebastea, part of the Eastern Empire, in 1059. It was written by the chronicler, Matthew of Edessa, early in the 12th century.

C **SOURCE**

One of the pilgrims was a noble abbess. Against all advice she went on a pilgrimage to the Holy Land. But she was captured by pagans and, in sight of all, was raped by a band of Turks until she died. This event was a scandal to all Christian people.

From a Christian chronicle, 'The Life of Bishop Altmann of Passau'.

A **SOURCE**

The Dome of the Rock, the most famous of the Muslim mosques in Jerusalem.

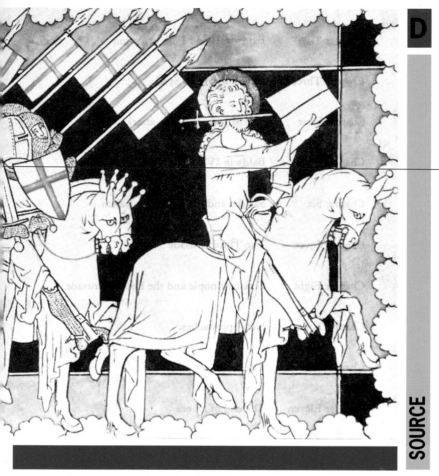

Crusading knights being led into battle by Christ.

Christians, hurry to help your brothers who live in the east, for they are being attacked. The Turks are killing them and ravaging the Kingdom of God. Arm for the rescue of Jerusalem under your captain Christ. Wear His cross as your badge. If you die your sins will be pardoned and you will go straight to Heaven.

Part of Urban's speech, according to Fulcher of Chartres. He was a chaplain who was at Clermont and went on the First Crusade. He wrote his account in 1105.

Pope Urban thought it would be a good idea to get men from all parts of the Christian world to travel to the east and fight the Turks. This would help Alexius, but what Urban really wanted was to win back the Holy City of Jerusalem from the Muslims. He made an appeal for soldiers in a famous speech at Clermont in France, in 1095.

As Urban finished his speech the crowd shouted 'Deus le Volt' (God wills it). Men began to volunteer for the campaign. They cut out red crosses and sewed them on their clothes as a sign that they were fighting for Christ. The French for cross is 'croix' and soon men talked of going on the 'croisades'. In England they were called **Crusades** – wars fought on behalf of the Pope to recover the Holy Land.

In 1096 the First Crusade set off. Little did these first crusaders realize that their campaign would be just one of many to leave Europe over the next 300 years.

Urban II

Urban II (?1042–99), christened Otto, went to the cathedral school in Rheims. He joined the monastery at Cluny and became Prior of Cluny in about 1076. Two years later Otto was invited to Rome by Pope Gregory VII and was made Cardinal-bishop of Ostia. Otto became one of the Pope's closest advisors.

In March 1088 Otto was unanimously elected as Pope and took the name Urban II. He was the person who contributed most to organizing the First Crusade. As Pope, he persuaded Christian rulers who often fought each other to work together.

2.2 Who Went?

Pope Urban's appeal for soldiers to fight for Jerusalem was a success. All over Europe great nobles, clergy and peasants began preparing for the trip. It was no easy task. Ahead of the crusaders lay a journey of over 1,500 miles through little-known and possibly dangerous lands.

So many of the clergy wanted to go that Urban said they had to get permission first. He also said that the Church would look after people's property while they were away. Urban announced that all crusaders' sins would be forgiven – but only if they got as far as the Church of the Holy Sepulchre.

The crusading forces came from many different parts of Europe. Their leaders had a variety of reasons for going on the crusade. But above all else they strongly believed that it was God's will that the Holy Land should be won back for Christianity.

One of the leaders was Raymond of St Giles, Count of Toulouse, in France. He was 60 years old and nearing the end of his life, but was determined to win glory in the eyes of God before his death. Before he left France, Raymond gave away much of his property to the monastery of St Giles. He swore an oath saying he intended to stay in the Holy Land until his death.

B SOURCE

Oh what pain! What sighs! What weeping! What sadness when a husband left his beloved wife and children and whatever possessions he had.

Yet the crusaders were happy to leave all their possessions behind. They knew they would increase them a hundredfold as the Lord had promised. Grief it was to those who remained behind, but joy to those who left.

Written by the French chaplain, Fulcher of Chartres. He went on the First Crusade and recorded what he saw.

Illuminated page from a 13th-century Christian manuscript, 'The Crusades of Godfrey of Bouillon'.

A SOURCE

C SOURCE

Hundreds of less important nobles also went on the crusade. For them it meant risking financial ruin. Many of them had to sell or mortgage their land on very poor terms. They had to pay for weapons, armor, horses and equipment. They also had to pay their own travel costs and take large sums of money with them to pay for food and other expenses.

From 'The Crusades' by Z. Oldenbourg, 1966.

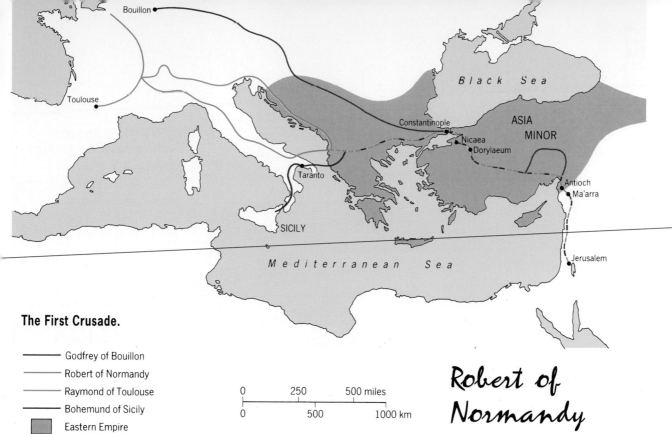

The First Crusade.

——— Godfrey of Bouillon
——— Robert of Normandy
——— Raymond of Toulouse
——— Bohemund of Sicily
▧ Eastern Empire

0	250	500 miles
0	500	1000 km

Robert of Normandy

Other important French nobles also brought forces on the crusade. Among them were Hugh, Count of Vermandois (the French king's youngest son), Robert of Normandy (William the Conqueror's son) and Stephen of Blois.

From Germany came Godfrey of Bouillon, Duke of Lorraine. He had already fought battles for Christianity against the Muslims. He was so determined to go on the crusade that he mortgaged his estates in order to equip his army. With him were his brothers, Eustace and Baldwin. Baldwin took his wife and children with him because he intended to live in the Holy Land. (Later, Baldwin became King of Jerusalem, but sadly by then his wife and children were already dead.)

The Normans who had conquered Sicily also sent a force under their leader Bohemund. The Eastern Emperor Alexius was disturbed to hear that Bohemund was coming. Bohemund and Alexius were enemies; they had fought each other in the past.

So in the autumn of 1096, several armies set out from different parts of Europe. By April 1097 they had all reached Alexius's capital, Constantinople. Their journeys had been long and difficult. But when they turned their attention to the Turks, life became even harder.

Robert of Normandy (?1054–1134) was the eldest son of William the Conqueror. His parents wanted him to inherit Normandy and made him regent for William in 1067. He was small and fat, so was often called 'Curthose' (referring to his short legs). He was also said to be generous and intelligent.

In 1087 he inherited Normandy, but wanted to be King of England too. He plotted against William Rufus. In 1096 he went on the First Crusade and fought with great bravery. In 1100 William Rufus died. His brother Henry became King of England. Robert tried to overthrow him, but was defeated at the Battle of Tinchebray in 1106.

Robert spent the rest of his life in prison. It is said he starved himself to death in 1134.

2.3 On the Road to Jerusalem

While the nobles of Europe were preparing their armies for the First Crusade, another force, the **People's Crusade**, was already on the road. From across Europe, more than 300,000 ordinary people came together to march to Jerusalem. Most of these people were simple peasants, though there were also some wealthier knights. Amazingly, they had little idea about what they were going to do when they got to the Holy Land. Their leader, the preacher **Peter the Hermit**, seems to have encouraged them to believe that the Turks would simply run away in fear at the sight of their force.

The People's Crusade got off to a bad start. They did not wait until they reached the Holy Land to begin what they saw as God's work. As they traveled eastwards through Europe they carried out terrible attacks on some Jewish communities on their route. Many Jewish men, women and children committed suicide to avoid being slaughtered. In Hungary the crusaders' behavior was so bad that the Hungarians attacked them. By the time the People's Crusade reached Constantinople, disease, starvation and attacks from hostile Europeans had reduced their number to less than 100,000.

Emperor Alexius took one look at the People's Crusade and decided that the sooner he got rid of it the better. So he quickly shipped them into Asia Minor to face the Turks. In September 1096 the People's Crusade was destroyed by the Turks at Nicaea. Most were killed, many of the survivors were sold into slavery. Peter the Hermit managed to return to Constantinople to beg for the Emperor's pardon.

By April 1097 the armies of the First Crusade had arrived in Constantinople. Alexius provided ships for them to cross into Turkish territory and in return they captured and gave him the Turkish town of Nicaea. Then they set off for Jerusalem. As the crusaders marched through the burning heat they were ambushed by the **Saracens** (as the crusaders called the Turkish Muslims). The Saracens also burned orchards and poisoned wells to prevent the crusaders from getting enough food and water. The crusaders were only able to fight back successfully when the Saracens made the mistake of fighting a full-scale battle with them. The crusaders were good at this type of fighting. One such success came at Dorylaeum in July 1097 – but even then the crusaders nearly lost.

A **SOURCE**

Since these men were advancing in no sort of order, they fell into Saracen ambushes and were miserably wiped out. Such a large number were slaughtered that their remains made not merely a hill or mound or peak, but a huge mountain, deep and wide, so great was the pile of bones.

The end of the People's Crusade. This was written around 1140 by Anna Comenus, daughter of the Emperor Alexius.

Emperor Alexius Commenus

Alexius Commenus (1048–1118) was head of the Eastern (Byzantine) Empire at the time of the First Crusade. He had fought well in battles to prevent the Turks taking over the Empire. In 1081, with the help of his mother and brother, he seized the throne from Emperor Nicephorus.

The Empire had been weakened by constant fighting with the Turks and the Normans. Alexius restored the Empire's power.

SOURCE

Victory for the crusaders at the Battle of Dorylaeum. From a 14th-century French manuscript.

In October 1097 the crusading armies reached Antioch, an important trading town. Many of the crusaders were very discouraged by the city's huge walls and large garrison. They wondered how they could ever take the city. After a nine-month siege, Antioch was finally taken when one of the city's leaders was bribed to let the crusaders in. But the crusading forces soon quarreled over which of their leaders should have the city. Then a new army of Saracens arrived and laid siege to Antioch. Soon the crusaders began to run out of food. People were reduced to eating leaves off the trees. Many of them were ready to surrender.

According to legend it was at this point that the Holy Lance was found and the crusaders fought off the Saracens. Whatever the truth of this story, the crusaders stopped their squabbling and prepared to march on Jerusalem.

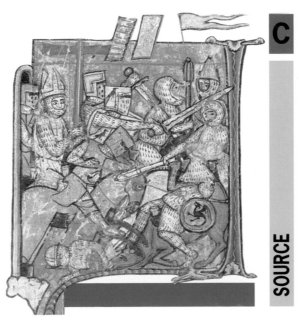

C

SOURCE

D

A poor priest told them that he had seen a vision. He said that St Andrew had told him that the Holy Lance which once pierced Christ's side was buried in the Cathedral at Antioch. Whoever had this lance would gain victory. Soon soldiers were busily digging in the cathedral. When they found the lance they danced with joy. The Christians then went and destroyed the Saracens.

SOURCE

From 'Know about the Crusades' by H. Treece, 1963.

The Holy Lance, carried in battle at Antioch by Adhemar, Bishop of Le Puy. From a 13th-century Christian manuscript.

2.4 The Siege of Jerusalem

Just before the crusaders left Antioch, the Bishop of Le Puy, the official leader of the forces, died. This caused yet another fight among the nobles about who should be the new leader. When they set off for Jerusalem on 1 November 1098, both Bohemund and Raymond of Toulouse claimed to be in charge. Shortly after the crusaders captured the town of Ma'arra, however, Bohemund returned to Antioch and took over the city. He was quite prepared to let Raymond lead the crusade if he could have Antioch.

In January 1099 Raymond continued his march. He stopped to attack the town of Arqa, where he was soon joined by Godfrey of Bouillon and the other European nobles. They wanted to press on instead of attacking the city and another fight broke out. Raymond was supported by Peter Bartholomew, the monk who had first had the vision of the Holy Lance (see page 17, Source D). Some priests said that Bartholomew was a fraud and challenged him to submit to an ordeal by fire. To prove the lance genuine he must clasp it in his arms and hurl himself into a fire. Bartholomew accepted without hesitation, but died twelve days later in appalling agony. Fewer people believed in the lance now and most crusaders recognized Godfrey, not Raymond, as the new leader.

B SOURCE

The Saracens reacted to the march round Jerusalem by raising their own crosses on the city wall. Then they insulted the crusaders, spat on them and subjected them to outrages of which it is not decent to speak. The crusaders were determined to gain revenge for this.

From 'The Crusades' by Z. Oldenbourg, 1966.

C SOURCE

Tancred was searching for wood to build siege machines, but his dysentry was so bad that he had to keep getting off his horse to find a private place. He was troubled so often that he decided to give up the search. Then the trouble started again and he was forced to find peace in a place surrounded by trees and bushes. Good gracious! As he was relieving himself, he realized that he was facing a cave where four hundred timbers had been stored!

A lucky find of wood. Described by Radulph of Caen, a friend of Tancred who accompanied him on the crusades.

A SOURCE

The crusaders attack the walls of Jerusalem. A siege machine can be clearly seen. From a 14th-century French manuscript.

Crusaders loot the captured city of Jerusalem. From a 15th-century French manuscript.

So the march continued. On 7 June 1099 the crusaders at last reached Jerusalem. We are told that when the army finally came within sight of the great walls and towers of the city they wept with joy. But their task was by no means over. Jerusalem had very solid defenses and a strong garrison of Saracens. The crusaders found it very difficult to capture the city. They did not really have the equipment necessary to break through the strong walls. They needed wood to build **siege machines** which they could use to knock down the walls, but there was very little wood to be found.

Then one of the priests had a vision saying that if the soldiers marched three times round the city barefoot they would capture it within nine days. This they did on 8 July and five days later they launched a fierce attack. Soon they broke through the walls. In the next two days they took control of the city. Once inside the walls the crusaders behaved with great cruelty towards the inhabitants. They shut up many Jews in their synagogue, and then set it on fire. They slaughtered any Muslim they met. It has been estimated that as many as 40,000 men, women and children were cut down by the crusaders' swords in just two days. The massacre filled the entire Muslim world with horror. Yet the recapture of Jerusalem was greeted in the Christian world with great joy.

Our soldiers chased the Saracens as far as the Temple of Solomon. There, a good number of men and women were captured and put to death. Their blood flowed all over the temple.

Our army seized gold, silver, horses and mules and riches of all kinds. Then they came rejoicing and weeping for joy to worship at the Church of the Holy Sepulchre.

In the morning our men climbed onto the roof of the temple and beheaded the Saracen men and women who were hiding there.

From the 'Gesta Francorum' by an anonymous European chronicler who witnessed the fall of Jerusalem.

Bohemund of Antioch

Bohemund of Antioch (?1050–1111) was the son of a Norman mercenary knight. He was nicknamed 'Bohemund' after a legendary giant. He and Alexius, the Eastern Emperor, were bitter enemies for nearly thirty years, but he was persuaded to join in the First Crusade with Alexius by the Pope, Urban II.

In 1098 Bohemund became ruler of Antioch. He took every chance to ally with other rulers. He had many meetings with the Pope. In 1106 he married the daughter of Philip I of France.

2.5 The Crusader States

Once the crusaders had defeated the Saracens they decided to divide the conquered lands between them. This included Jerusalem, Antioch and Edessa, which Godfrey's cousin, Baldwin, ruled. Soon they had control of Tripoli as well. These four areas became known as the **crusader states**, though the Saracens called them the **Frankish states**. To the Saracens all Christians were '**Franks**'.

The new states were not all of equal importance. Jerusalem soon became a kingdom and claimed to have overlordship of the other three states. Its first ruler was Godfrey, but he did not want to be known as a king. Instead he called himself 'Guardian of the Holy Sepulchre'. When Godfrey died, his brother Baldwin accepted the title 'King of Jerusalem'. The leaders of the other states had various titles – Count of Tripoli, Count of Edessa and Prince of Antioch.

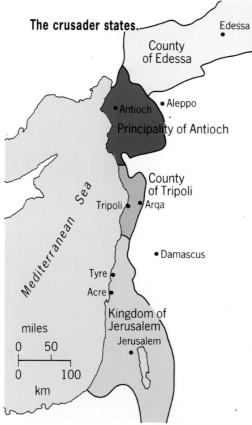

The crusader states.

Although the crusaders controlled these four areas, they did not own all the cities in them. They had to fight many battles to keep control. Many of the crusaders had gone home after the capture of Jerusalem, so the remaining crusader forces were small. Sometimes, in order to survive, they even made alliances with Saracen leaders to help fight their enemies. The Christian Count of Tripoli had local Muslim allies called 'Assassins' who were said to smoke hashish and murder anyone their leader told them to! Yet the crusaders continued to advance. In 1124 they captured the city of Tyre. This gave them control of almost all the important places along the coast of the Holy Land.

Baldwin of Flanders

Baldwin of Flanders (1172–1205) wa Count of Flanders and Hainaut. He helped the English fight the French and fought with Richard I against Philip Augustus of France.

He helped capture Constantinople in the Fourth Crusade and became rule of part of the city in 1204.

A Frank playing chess with a Saracen.

C

SOURCE

Without delay he summoned the cook and made him swear an oath. On the king's death the cook was to cut open his stomach and throw away his internal organs. Then he had to rub salt inside and outside the body and put spices and basalm in the eyes, mouth, nostrils and ears. Once this was done Baldwin was to be wrapped in hangings and tied firmly on his horse. That way he could be taken home to Jerusalem for a Christian burial – and the enemy would not even know he was dead.

Albert of Aachen tells of the orders given by Baldwin as he lay dying during a campaign to Egypt in 1118. Albert was a German chronicler who recorded the stories of pilgrims on their return from the crusades.

D

SOURCE

became ruler of Jerusalem and set a new system of government, sed on the Norman feudal system. hundred knights were given land und Constantinople after swearing hs of allegiance to Baldwin. dwin led an army against Kayolan Bulgaria in 1205 but was captured d executed.

The rulers of the new states tried to govern as they had at home. They imposed the **feudal system** of governing, where the king gave rewards to barons who swore allegiance to him. Then knights swore allegiance to the barons, and so on down to the peasants. The new rulers also introduced a church organization like the one at home. Patriarchs (church leaders) were set up in Antioch and Jerusalem. Below them were archbishops, bishops, abbots and priors. Merchants also flocked into the Holy Land. They realized that there were great profits to be made from trading in rich tapestries and delicacies.

The Franks could not really hope to live in the East in the same way as they had done in the West. For a start, western-style clothes were unsuitable in the great heat. So the Franks began to wear eastern styles of dress, such as robes and turbans. Many of the women began to wear veils like Muslim women – though probably this was just to keep the fierce sun off their faces. The Franks also built their houses in eastern styles and decorated them with local tapestries and furniture.

As the crusaders settled down to live in peace with the Saracens they came to realize how wrong they had been to call them barbarians. Many Saracens, too, were surprised at just how civilized the 'western devils' were. Before long, inter-marriage between the two races became quite common. When enthusiastic pilgrims arrived from Europe they were often amazed to discover that the old crusaders were happy to live in peace with the Saracens, rather than fight them.

3.1 The Second Crusade, 1145–49

In the first half of the 12th century, the crusaders called the new states **'Outremer'**– the land across the sea. Generally the Franks lived on good terms with the Saracens, though there were still fierce battles and great cruelty towards prisoners captured by either side.

However, on Christmas Day 1144, disaster struck the crusaders when the Saracen leader, **Zanghi**, captured the city of Edessa. Soon the rest of the State of Edessa was in Saracen hands. When Zanghi died in 1146, Nureddin became their leader.

With the fall of Edessa, the kingdom of Jerusalem was in real danger – especially as its king, Baldwin III, was too young to lead the Frankish forces. His mother, Queen Melisende, appealed to Pope Eugenius for help. The Pope was determined to prevent a repeat of earlier disasters like the People's Crusade. So he sent an abbot called Bernard to appeal directly to the kings of Europe for help. Bernard was a very powerful speaker. The Holy Roman Emperor, **Conrad III,** and **Louis VII of France**, agreed to bring forces to save Jerusalem.

In 1147 the two kings set off along the route taken by the First Crusaders. Conrad was the first to arrive in Constantinople in September 1147. Louis arrived one month later. The Eastern Emperor, Manuel, was not particularly pleased to see them – especially as he knew of the trouble the crusaders of 1096 had caused.

B SOURCE

Some were struck down with stones, some with javelins, and many were mutilated in different ways. Watching this, the wicked heathen leader was delighted by their torments and he laughed at them.

The massacre of Christian prisoners taken at the Battle of Aleppo in 1119. Written by Walter the Chancellor who was at the battle.

C SOURCE

Zanghi ordered the murdering to stop. He appointed good men to govern the city. He gave the inhabitants promises of good government and justice. Indeed every region and town he passed through was immediately handed over to him.

How Zanghi won over the people of Edessa. Described in the 'Damascus Chronicle' written by a Muslim chronicler between 1140 and 1160.

D SOURCE

The reputation of the Franks was crushed to the earth. From now on the unclean nations, who had been in terror of the Franks, were able to laugh at them.

William, Archbishop of Tyre, describes the effect of the defeat on the crusaders' reputation. William was born in Jerusalem in 1130 and was the official historian of King Almanc I of Jerusalem.

A SOURCE

Christian prisoners being beheaded by Saracens. It was common for crusaders and Saracens to behead their prisoners. From a 14th-century French manuscript.

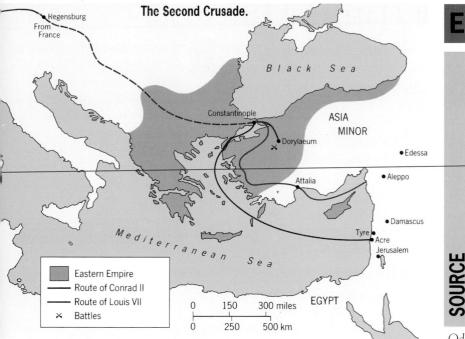

The Second Crusade.

Regensburg
From France

Black Sea

Constantinople

ASIA MINOR

Dorylaeum

• Edessa

Attalia

• Aleppo

• Damascus

Tyre
Acre
Jerusalem

M e d i t e r r a n e a n   S e a

EGYPT

	Eastern Empire
	Route of Conrad II
	Route of Louis VII
×	Battles

0   150   300 miles
0   250   500 km

Manuel helped the crusaders cross into Asia Minor, but both the Germans and the French soon met with disaster. Conrad's forces did not take enough food with them. His hungry army became so weak that it was easily defeated at the Battle of Dorylaeum. Some sources say that Conrad lost nine-tenths of his army in the battle. Conrad was forced to return to Constantinople with the survivors, where he met up with Louis' army. Louis' men had undergone a terrible journey. Thousands had died from disease, starvation or Saracen attacks.

Eventually Conrad and Louis hired ships and completed their journey by sea. But many of Louis' men were left behind to die in Asia Minor. In June 1148 the two kings met Baldwin III and his mother at Acre. They decided to capture Damascus and prevent the Saracen forces from joining up with fellow Muslims from Egypt. It was a brave plan, but a foolish one. The crusader forces were not strong enough to capture the city. The different armies also distrusted each other and their leaders argued during the campaign. After a five-day attack they were forced to retreat with heavy losses. The people of Damascus, who until this time had been friendly with the crusaders, now told the Saracen leader Nureddin that they would support him.

Conrad and Louis returned to their own countries after the defeat at Damascus, though Louis did stay in the Holy Land until the following summer. He was determined that if he could not be a successful crusader, he would at least be a successful pilgrim.

Louis VII

Louis VII of France (1120–80) became King of France in 1137. He and Pope Innocent II argued. Louis was excommunicated. In 1145 he went on the Second Crusade hoping Innocent would forgive him. But the crusade was not successful.

Louis was married three times. The first two wives did not have children. The third wife, Alix of Champagne, had a son, Philip Augustus, in 1165. Philip became king when Louis died in 1180.

3.2 The Battle of Hattin, 1187

The failure of the Second Crusade made many people in western Europe question whether such campaigns really did any good. So it was more than 40 years before another crusade set off – and it took the fall of Jerusalem to bring it about.

Jerusalem had remained under threat from the Saracens since the Second Crusade. Messengers regularly came from the city to Europe asking for help. Things became so bad that in 1165 Pope Alexander III called for a crusade. But the kings of Europe were too tied up in their own squabbles to risk such a dangerous expedition.

The rulers of western Europe didn't realize that the Saracens were gaining strength in the Holy Land. Their new leader, **Saladin**, now controlled a wide area of land bordering on the Christian states. He made peace with the King of Jerusalem, but another Frankish noble, Reynald of Chatillon, broke the peace terms. He attacked a group of Saracen pilgrims in which Saladin's sister was traveling. Saladin retaliated by capturing the town of Tiberias. In 1187 **King Guy of Jerusalem** tried to win Tiberias back. Although the Christian leaders did not all agree, it was decided to march to Hattin, near Tiberias, and attack Saladin's army.

When Saladin heard that Guy was moving towards Tiberias, he ordered his troops to retreat to the edge of a nearby lake. He knew that Guy's troops were short of water and that this would affect their ability to fight. To weaken the Frankish forces further, Saladin ordered his archers to attack them as they marched.

B SOURCE

Nobody has ever denied that the Battle of Hattin had a decisive impact on the history of the crusader states in the Holy Land. Hattin led to Saladin's conquest of nearly all the lands held by the Franks, including his occupation of Jerusalem on 2 October.

From the magazine 'History Today', March 1987.

C SOURCE

So many were slain, wounded or thrown in chains that our people were a pitiful sight, even to the enemy. Even worse, the True Cross was taken into the hands of our enemy.

Description of the battle in the 'Itinerarium', an account written by a monk in London around 1200. The True Cross was believed to part of the cross on which Christ died. It was discovered in Jerusalem in 1099 by the first crusaders.

A SOURCE

The defeat of the Franks at Hattin. Saladin is seen seizing the True Cross. From a 13th-century English manuscript.

The Count of Tripoli said, 'Tiberias belongs to me. If Saladin takes the town and all my possessions and then goes away I shall be happy enough. I have never seen such a huge army. But if he takes the town he will not be able to stay there, because his army will not put up for long with being away from their homes and families. He will be forced to evacuate the city, and we will re-capture it and free our prisoners. There is no need to risk a battle.'

But Reynald angrily replied, 'You have tried hard to make us afraid of the Saracens. Clearly you take their side, otherwise you would not have spoken in this way. As for the size of their army, a large load of fuel will be good for the fires of Hell.' So the generals decided to advance and give battle.

The Christian leaders discuss tactics. From an account by the Muslim chronicler Ibn al-Athir, who served in Saladin's army.

Guy of Jerusalem

Guy of Jerusalem (1129–94) was a French noble who, in 1180, married Sibyl, the sister of King Baldwin of Jerusalem. In 1186 Baldwin died and Guy became King of Jerusalem.

In 1187 Guy was defeated by Saladin at Hattin. He decided not to fight any further battles against the Saracens. But in 1190 he led a siege against the Saracen fort of Acre. It failed. In 1192 he gave the title of King of Jerusalem to Richard I of England in exchange for the island of Cyprus.

Saladin's tactics worked. When the battle began, Guy's infantry complained that they were dying of thirst and could not fight. His cavalry made several very brave charges and some of them managed to escape. But many were slaughtered. Both Guy and Reynald were taken prisoner. Saladin was so angry with Reynald that he personally cut off the nobleman's head. Now that the Frankish army had been destroyed, the crusader states lay defenceless before Saladin's army.

It did not take Saladin long to follow up his victory at the Battle of Hattin. Castles and cities sometimes surrendered at the very sight of his huge army. Only the strongest of the castles, like that at **Krak des Chevaliers**, managed to survive. **Acre**, the second most important city in the crusader states, surrendered without even putting up a fight. On 2 October Saladin won his biggest prize – Jerusalem.

Jerusalem was defended by a very small force. It was said that there were 50 women and children for every man in the city. Fortunately for them, Saladin was prepared to accept a deal. Those who could afford to pay a ransom he let go free; those who could not pay were sold into slavery. The Saracens then occupied the city, but there was none of the butchery that had been seen when the crusaders first took Jerusalem in 1099. Saladin acted with restraint. His advisers told him to destroy the Church of the Holy Sepulchre, but he refused. Within three days he let Christian pilgrims visit the city – as long as they paid a fee.

The great castle of Krak des Chevaliers.

3.3 Sultan Saladin

Sultan Saladin was respected by friend and foe alike. Today he is one of the heroes of Arab history – the great leader who saved Jerusalem from the Christians. Yet it is not only the Arabs who admired him. He lived at a time when most Christians considered all Arabs to be inferior. But many of them praised Saladin's character. What was so special about this man?

A portrait of Saladin painted by an Egyptian artist some years after Saladin's death.

An army scout brought a French woman to Saladin. She wept with grief. Saladin asked what was wrong and she said, 'Yesterday some Muslim thieves entered my tent and stole my little girl. I cried all night and our commanders told me, "the King of the Muslims is merciful," so I came to ask for my daughter back.'

Saladin was touched and tears came to his eyes. He sent someone to the slave market to fetch the girl. When she was returned the mother wept with joy. She and the daughter were escorted back to the French camp.

A story about Saladin by Baha-ad-Din Ibn Shaddad, a Muslim historian who lived at Saladin's court.

A portrait of Saladin by a French artist in the 19th century.

Saladin fighting Richard I. This contest never actually took place.

Saladin

Prince Reynald was led into the presence of Saladin. Out of either rage or envy of the excellence of the man, that tyrant cut off with his own hand that veteran old head. He also ordered to be beheaded all the Templars who were taken. He wished to kill off those whom he knew to be braver than all others in battle.

From the 'Itinerarium', an account written by a monk in London around 1200.

Saladin (?1137–93), Yussuf Salah–ad–Din in Arabic, was the son of a Kurdish chief. He was a skilled soldier, but did not enjoy campaigning.

In 1175 Saladin became the Sultan of Egypt and decided to reconquer all Muslim lands, including the Holy Land. He captured Syria, then attacked the crusaders in the Holy Land. In 1187, he inflicted a crushing defeat on them at the Battle of Hattin. Later in the same year he captured the city of Jerusalem.

This extraordinary man's behavior was anything but saintly. He was not incapable of cruelty or cheating. He was calculating, cold and unscrupulous. He managed to put a good face on even his most questionable actions.

From 'The Crusades' by Z. Oldenbourg, 1966.

In 1189 Richard I of England and Philip II of France launched a Third Crusade against Saladin. But they could not defeat him. With much weaker forces, Saladin prevented the crusaders from retaking Jerusalem. In 1192 Richard returned to England. Saladin returned to his capital at Damascus and four months later died of yellow fever.

Saladin was a great warrior, but he was not rough and unmannerly. In fact the Arabs had strict rules about the treatment of guests. Even among a people with such standards of good manners, Saladin stood out and was famous for his courtesy. To the Arabs, the crusaders must have seemed rough and barbarous.

From 'Pilgrimages and Crusades' by G. Evans, 1976.

3.4 The Third Crusade, 1189–92

Saladin's capture of Jerusalem shocked the western world. Pope Urban III is said to have died of grief when he heard the news! People could not understand how God could have allowed the Holy City to fall once more into the hands of the Saracens. They believed it was a punishment from God for their sins; they thought a new crusade would help make up for their wrong-doings. In 1189 three of Europe's kings raised forces to go to the Holy Land. From France came **Philip II**, from Germany the **Emperor Frederick Barbarossa** (so called because he had a red beard) and from England **Richard 'the Lionheart'**.

In May 1189 Barbarossa set out, taking a land route similar to the one taken by the previous two crusades. He encountered many of the same problems. The Eastern Emperor refused to give supplies and banned his people from providing food to the crusaders. Barbarossa pressed on into Asia Minor, but when he was within a few days march of Antioch, disaster struck. As he bathed in the river Gorlu, Barbarossa was drowned. Many of his soldiers were so upset that they returned home. Only a fraction of the original army made it to the Holy Land.

Barbarossa's death was a bitter blow to the crusade, because both Richard and Philip would probably have accepted him as leader. As it was, these two spent much of their time arguing. Neither was even prepared to say that he would go on the crusade until the other one did! They were both frightened that their kingdoms would be attacked while they were away.

An anonymous 12th-century chronicler, commenting on the reasons for the fall of Jerusalem.

The Arab chronicler, Ibn al-Athir, describes Barbarossa's death. Ibn al-Athir served in Saladin's army.

A | **SOURCE**

Philip and Richard, seen here quarreling in Sicily. From a 14th-century French manuscript.

Eventually both kings did set off, traveling by sea rather than overland. Their journey was very slow. They spent the winter in Sicily, the spring in Cyprus and did not arrive in Acre until early summer 1191.

At Acre they met Guy of Jerusalem. He had been taken prisoner at the Battle of Hattin, but had been released by Saladin on the condition that he did not renew the war. Guy considered that the promise had been forced from him and that it did not count. So he had gathered a new army and laid siege to Acre.

The arrival of Richard and Philip strengthened the Frankish forces and they soon took the city. But it was a long and costly siege, with heavy losses on both sides. Still Philip and Richard quarreled. They had both been ill with typhoid during the siege, but since Richard had been less ill, he had led the army. Philip decided that capturing Acre was enough and returned home. Some said that he really went because he was jealous of Richard's popularity with both English and French soldiers.

Richard set off for Jerusalem. But it was now the height of the summer and many of his soldiers became ill with the heat. Despite this, Richard won a great victory at Arsuf and recaptured Jaffa. Yet he never made it to Jerusalem. In the spring of 1192 he heard news that he was needed in England. So he signed a three-year truce with Saladin and set sail for home.

Frederick I

Frederick I (1123–90) was elected as Holy Roman Emperor in 1152. During his time as Emperor relations with the Papacy were often strained. In 1153 he signed the Treaty of Constance with Pope Eugenius III. In this treaty the Pope agreed to stop the Eastern Emperor taking land in Italy. But the next Pope, Adrian, broke the agreement. In 1159 Frederick helped Pope Victor IV to be elected as Pope. Other countries supported Alexander III. Alexander retired to France for a while in 1161, having excommunicated Frederick. When Alexander returned to Rome, Frederick sent four separate armies against him, but was finally defeated at Legnano in 1176. Fredrick finally acknowledged Alexander as the true Pope.

In 1189 Frederick set off on the Third Crusade to free Jerusalem from Saladin's control. In 1190, within just a few day's march of Antioch, Frederick was drowned in the River Gorlu.

From the 'Itinerarium', an account written by a monk living in London around 1200. He is commenting on Philip's decision to return home.

E **SOURCE**

A contemporary drawing of the Emperor Barbarossa.

3.5 The Siege of Acre, 1189–91

In August 1189 **King Guy of Jerusalem** began besieging the town of **Acre**. His force contained not only Franks from the Holy Land, but also crusaders from Italy and (later) Denmark and Holland. Saladin tried to break the siege by attacking Guy's forces, but was unable to do so. Instead he settled for besieging the forces who were besieging Acre! Soon Guy's forces were suffering terrible food shortages. They seemed to have little chance of capturing the city.

In the summer of 1191 fresh forces arrived by sea, led by King Richard of England and King Philip of France. They brought not only fresh troops, but also new fighting techniques. Now that the Franks had a fleet they could prevent the city being supplied from the sea. Soon they captured a ship from Beirut, packed with supplies.

The new forces brought with them the latest ideas in **siege warfare**. A huge catapult called 'God's Own Catapult' began to hurl heavy rocks against the city walls. The crusaders dug under the city walls and lit fires to bring them crashing down. The people in the city knew that these forces were too strong for them and too strong for Saladin to defeat. The only option was to give in. The city surrendered on 12 July 1191. Acre then became the Franks' new capital in the Holy Land, until Jerusalem could be recaptured.

During the siege, Richard made a mistake which was to cost his kingdom dearly in the next few years.

A I weep and am deeply grieved to report that our army has given itself over to disgraceful pursuits and indulgences in idleness and lust instead of the practice of virtue. The Lord is not present in the camp and there is no one there who does good. The commanders are jealous of each other and the lower ranks are short of provisions. Purity, faith, love and charity are missing from the camp. As God is my witness, I should hardly believe it had I not seen it with my own eyes.

SOURCE

Account of the behavior of Guy's army outside Acre in 1190, as witnessed by the chaplain of the Archbishop of Canterbury.

B Priceless horses were slaughtered so that men could eat. Horse's guts were sold for ten shillings. Even noblemen would fall on their knees and eat plants. Some men were seen running about like mad dogs, desperate with hunger. If they found bones thrown out and gnawed by dogs three days ago, they would sieze them, gnawing where there was nothing left to gnaw at, suck and lick them. Not that they got anything, except the pleasure of gnawing at the memory of meat.

SOURCE

Account of the hunger of the besieging Christian forces. From the 'Itinerarium', written by a monk in London around 1200.

C Their leaders offered to surrender the city of Acre, hand back the Holy Cross and free two hundred and fifty noble Christian captives. When our men said this was not enough, they offered two thousand nobles and five hundred humbler prisoners, whom Saladin ordered to be sought throughout the land. In addition they were to pay two hundred thousand sovereigns. Until these terms were met three thousand Saracen soldiers were to be kept as hostages.

SOURCE

Terms of the surrender of the city. From the 'Itinerarium'.

Richard and Philip raised their standards on the wall of Acre. **Duke Leopold of Austria,** whose soldiers also took part in the siege, put his standard up too. Richard told his men to take Leopold's standard down. Who was he, a mere duke, to place his standard beside those of kings! Leopold was insulted by this action. He hated Richard for what he had done and longed for revenge.

Once Acre was taken, Philip and Richard divided the city between them. Philip then returned home while Richard agreed the terms of the surrender with Saladin. But Saladin did not keep his side of the bargain quickly enough for Richard. On 29 August some 2,700 Saracen hostages were massacred.

In October 1192, problems in England forced Richard to return home. On his way across the Adriatic Sea, his ship was wrecked in a storm and he was forced to continue his journey by land. Unfortunately for him, this involved crossing the lands of **Leopold of Austria**! When Leopold heard that Richard was in his territory, he saw his chance to get his own back for the insult at Acre. Richard was captured and thrown into jail. Leopold only let him go after a huge ransom had been paid by the people of England.

E

SOURCE

When Saladin delayed in carrying out the agreement, Richard was angry and had the Saracen hostages slaughtered with lances and swords. Some people say he did this because he had decided to attack Ascalon and did not want to leave a large number of enemy soldiers in Acre.

Baha ad-Din describes the slaughter of the hostages. Baha ad-Din was a Muslim historian who lived at Saladin's court.

Richard I

Richard I (1157–99) became King of England in 1189.

In 1191 Richard (called 'the Lionheart' for his bravery), after over a year of negotiations, joined Philip II of France on the Third Crusade to the Holy Land. On his way back to England from the crusade, in 1192, he was captured by Leopold of Austria and handed over to the Holy Roman Emperor Henry VI. He spent two years as a prisoner and was released only after a huge ransom had been paid. He died in 1199 while campaigning against Philip II in France.

D

SOURCE

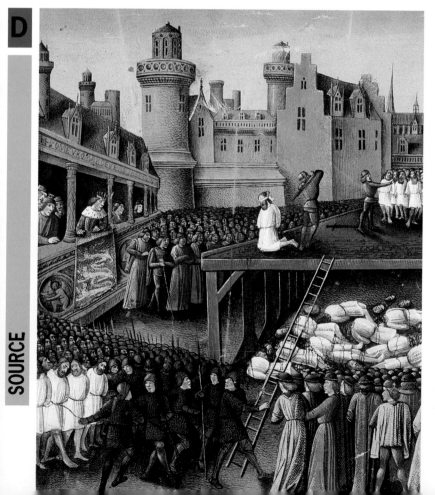

Richard watching the massacre of the Saracen prisoners. From a medieval Frankish manuscript.

3.6 The Fourth Crusade, 1202–4

In 1198 **Pope Innocent III** called for a crusade. He hoped that this would help stop the quarreling between the two Christian Churches: the western Catholic Church based in Rome and the eastern (or Greek Orthodox) Church based in Constantinople.

The leaders of the new crusade came mostly from France and Flanders. They were barons and knights. No kings went on this crusade. To get enough ships to sail to the Holy Land, the crusaders approached the Venetians. They were prepared to provide ships but they asked a high price. The crusaders couldn't raise enough money, so the Venetians asked them to capture the Hungarian town of **Zara** instead. This city was a trading rival of Venice. But it was also a Christian city and the Pope told them not to attack it. The crusaders felt they had no choice. They attacked and captured the town.

The original plan of the crusaders had been to attack Muslim **Egypt**. If they could establish control there, then they would deprive the Saracens of both the fine Egyptian fleet and their main source of grain. But the time taken in capturing Zara meant that any campaign would have to wait for better weather in the spring of 1203. Then a new plan was put to the crusaders.

The Eastern Emperor, Isaac, had recently been overthrown by his enemies in **Constantinople**. Isaac's son, Alexius, was on the crusade. He said that if the crusaders restored his father to the throne, then he would make sure that the Greek forces of the Eastern Empire helped the crusaders attack Egypt.

Some of the crusaders said that attacking Christian Constantinople was wrong. They should push on to Egypt without delay. Others pointed out how useful the Greek forces would be. The Venetians were delighted at the new idea. Their biggest trade rival was Constantinople and they also had valuable trade agreements with Egypt! A change of plan to attack the city and not Egypt would suit them nicely.

The leaders of the crusade decided to help Isaac. Some of the French were so disgusted by this that they went home. Others made their own way to the Holy Land. But the majority of the forces moved on to attack Constantinople. In June 1203 they broke into the city. Isaac was restored to the throne as joint Emperor with Alexius and the crusaders left the city.

Then the Abbot said, 'In the name of the Pope, I forbid you to attack this city. The people in it are Christians and you wear the sign of the cross.'

The Doge turned to the crusade leaders and said, 'You have given me your promise, and now I call on you to keep your word.'

One of the leading French knights, Geoffrey of Villehardouin, writing shortly after the Fourth Crusade, describes the debate over attacking Zara.

The agreement reached between the Venetians and the crusaders.

Venice in the 14th century, from a contemporary French manuscript. The bronze horses at the front of St Mark's Cathedral were stolen from Constantinople by the Venetians.

There was so much treasure heaped up in Constantinople, so many precious gold and silver vessels, cloth of gold and rich jewels, that it was a wonder to behold. Never since the beginning of the world has such wealth been won.

Account of Robert of Clari, a French knight who witnessed the looting of Constantinople.

The Greeks may well hate us as dogs. These defenders of Christ who should have turned their sword against the Saracens have waded through Christian blood.

Pope Innocent III commenting shortly after the capture of Constantinople.

But Alexius could not keep his promises to the crusaders. He could not raise enough money to pay off the Venetians, nor could he get his people to agree to fight against the Saracens. Then Alexius and his father were murdered by fellow Greeks. This gave the crusaders, backed by the Pope, a good excuse to take over the city. It seemed that the crusade was now against Christian Constantinople, not against the Saracens!

So in April 1204 the crusaders carried out a second attack on the city. For three days the soldiers ran riot, forgetting their oaths not to harm women or attack churches or monasteries. Constantinople was shared out. Baldwin of Flanders, one of the leaders of the crusade, became Emperor and was given a quarter of the city. The Venetians and the crusaders divided the rest of Constantinople between them. The city was very wealthy and enormous amounts of booty were shared out between the new rulers.

The crusaders had become rich and Constantinople was now part of the Western Empire. But within 60 years the city was recaptured by the Greeks and re-established as the head of the Eastern Empire. The Greek Orthodox Church refused to submit to the Pope, and blamed him for what had happened. For centuries, hatred of the Catholic Church was common in the east.

Pope Innocent III

Pope Innocent III (1161–1216) established the idea that a pope could tell Catholic rulers how to behave.

He also called for crusades against the Muslims in Jerusalem (the Fourth Crusade) and against the Albigenses in France (the Albigensian Crusade). In 1206 he appointed Stephen Langton as Archbishop of Canterbury against the wishes of the King of England, King John. When King John complained, Innocent III excommunicated him.

3.7 The Children's Crusade, 1212

The Fourth Crusade had proved to be a dreadful embarrassment for western Europe. Hardly any of its crusaders had even reached the Holy Land. Most of their time was spent attacking the Christians of the Eastern Empire instead of the Saracens in Jerusalem. The greed of those who went on the Fourth Crusade was a far cry from the religious ideals of the early crusaders.

Yet events in 1212 showed that there were still many people who believed that with God's support the Holy City could be reclaimed from the Saracens. In that year two separate groups set out for Jerusalem. One group came from France and the other from Germany. Both of these crusading 'armies' were composed almost entirely of **young children**. They were convinced that God would guide them to the Holy Land and bring them victory against the Saracen armies. In many ways their unswerving faith was similar to that of those who went on the People's Crusade. The results were even more disastrous.

A

SOURCE

Two shepherd boys. A carving from Chartres Cathedral in France. We have no pictures of any of the child crusaders, but many of them must have looked like the children in this medieval carving.

The main driving force behind the French crusade seems to have been a 12-year-old shepherd, **Stephen of Cloyes**. Like all peasant children at this time, Stephen would not have been able to read or write. He would have spent most of his time in the hills tending his flock of sheep. Yet in May 1212 this simple peasant boy is said to have turned up at the court of King Philip of France claiming that he had a letter from Christ telling him to organize a crusade. King Philip was not impressed and told him to come back when he was older.

But Stephen was a determined boy. He was so convinced that he was doing God's work that he began preaching about going on a crusade to large crowds of children that gathered to hear him. He told them that they should march to the Holy Land. When they came to the sea, God would roll the waves back, just as he had done for the Israelites in the Bible. His story sounded so exciting that by June, 30,000 children had gathered in the French town of Vendôme. Most of them were aged between 11 and 15 years old; few of them had any idea of where the Holy Land was or the difficulties that lay ahead of them.

As the children marched south to Marseilles, they were greeted enthusiastically by the people of the towns on their route. Here at last was a truly innocent group of crusaders marching in God's name. These were not greedy knights out for what they could get, or proud kings trying to win glory – just children. In the Bible, the evil Herod had slaughtered innocent children in Bethlehem. How right it seemed that the children should now be going to win back the Holy Land.

The Church leaders weren't sure what to make of the **Children's Crusade**. Officially it never was a 'crusade' because the Pope did not give it his official blessing. However, the children were blessed by priests before they set off and some monks and priests accompanied them. Many must have hoped that the children's action would make the kings of Europe feel so guilty that they would organize another crusade of their own!

Many of the children were discouraged by the distances they had to walk. Every time they came to a big French town they hoped it was Jerusalem. The efforts of the march and the shortages of food and water caused some to turn back; others dropped dead with exhaustion. But eventually they reached Marseilles.

The children were disappointed to find that the sea did not part to allow them to walk across to the Holy Land. Instead they were forced to rely on two merchants, Hugh the Iron and William the Pig, who offered them free passage aboard their ships. The children crammed onto seven ships and they set off. It was nearly 20 years before anything was heard of them again. Then a young priest who had seen some of the children in Egypt returned to tell their tale.

Two of the seven ships had been wrecked off the coast of Sardinia and all the passengers had drowned. The other five had been captured by pirates who sold the children in the slave markets of Algeria and Egypt. Some people believe that Hugh the Iron and William the Pig had come to an arrangement with the pirates even before the ships set sail. They knew that fair European children would fetch good prices as slaves in the East. We can never be really sure what happened to the children. But there is no record of any of them ever returning home.

At the same time as Stephen was organizing the crusade in France, **German** children were also preparing for a crusade. Their leader, a boy called **Nicholas**, preached a message very similar to Stephen's. But the 20,000 German children in his party were probably older. There were also a larger number of girls and unmarried women in the German crusade than in the French one, along with many clergymen.

The German children had a much more difficult journey than the French. To reach the sea, they had to cross the Alps. Many of them died on the route or turned back. When they reached the Italian port of Genoa and discovered that the seas would not divide, thousands more decided to give up the crusade and settle where they were. Others pushed on to Rome to meet the Pope. He praised their bravery, but told them that they were too young to go on such a dangerous mission and that they should go home. So they began the exhausting march back to Germany. Only a few ever made it. Another group struggled to the port of Pisa, where they they boarded ships to the Holy Land. No one knows what happened to them.

Nicholas never returned home. His father was accused by other parents of encouraging Nicholas to carry out the crusade. They were so angry at the loss of their own children that they hanged him.

These double-crossing sea captains sailed the five remaining ships to Bougie and Alexandra and there sold all the children to Saracen noblemen and merchants. In the same year in which they were sold at a gathering of Saracen chiefs, eighteen children were slain in various ways. They were martyred because they were completely unwilling to give up the Christian faith.

An account of the fate of the children from the writings of the contemporary monk, Aubrey of Trois-Fontaines.

The children put us to shame. While we sleep they gladly go forth to conquer the Holy Land.

Pope Innocent III, commenting on the crusade after meeting some of the children.

An Arab slave market. Many of the young French crusaders were probably sold in markets like this.

The Children's Crusade is one of those incidents in history that today we find hard to understand – or even to believe. It is incredible to us that parents would allow such a thing to happen. The Children's Crusade tells us a lot about the attitudes of people of the time and how strong their religious beliefs were.

Philip II

Philip II (1165–1223) became King of France at the age of fifteen and ruled for forty-three years.

He is said to have been 'handsome, well-built, with a pleasant face, warm, with high color and a temperament disposed to good food, wine and women'. Certainly his liking for women caused him problems. He was excommunicated by the Pope for bigamy (marrying more than one woman at the same time) after marrying both Ingeborg of Denmark and Agnes of Meran after his first wife's death.

Philip spent much of his time fighting, either on the crusades or defending his right to rule France. He successfully defended his kingdom against attacks from Germans, Flemings and English, all in the year 1214! Philip and Richard I of England had a very difficult relationship. They spent much of the crusades trying to work together against Saladin, but they argued fiercely about how the wars should be fought and about who was in charge. While they were not fighting Saladin they were often fighting each other. Richard I died while in France fighting against Philip.

3.8 St Louis of France

King Louis IX of France has been described as a 'perfect medieval king'. He is said to have been kind and generous and a man whose life was guided by his strict religious beliefs. Less than 30 years after his death, King Louis was made a saint by the Roman Catholic Church.

Yet as a crusader Louis had no more success than those less worthy men who went before him. In 1249 he led a force to Egypt and managed to take the city of **Damietta**. The defending Muslim forces had heard a rumor that their leader was dead, so they abandoned the city. The Sultan was so angry at the premature announcement of his death that he had 50 officers strangled for their cowardice! After the victory at Damietta, Louis won a battle at **Mansourah** in 1250, but it cost the lives of half his cavalry. Louis was unable to make any more gains; soon disease and famine struck his army and forced him to retreat.

Louis' retreating forces were cut to pieces by the Muslims. It is estimated that up to 30,000 men died. Louis was taken prisoner. The price of his release was the return of Damietta to the Egyptians and 400,000 pieces of gold. Louis was scrupulously honest in paying this sum.

B **SOURCE**

Louis lived with a disregard for worldly vanities. He wore grey woolen cloth with fur only from deer-skin, hare-skin or lamb-skin. He had simple tastes in food and ate whatever was put before him. He always mixed water with his wine.

A description of Louis by John of Joinville, who served with Louis in the crusades and later wrote an account of Louis' life.

C **SOURCE**

In 1244 Louis was taken very seriously ill. He was so near to dying that one of the two ladies tending him wanted to draw the sheet over his face, maintaining that he was dead. But the other lady would not hear it. She was sure the soul was still in his body. As the King lay listening, the Lord worked within him and quickly brought him back to health. As soon as he was able, he asked for the cross to be brought to him. After the King had taken the cross, his example was followed by his three brothers and many others.

Joinville tells how Louis decided to go on a crusade.

A **SOURCE**

Louis taking the cross before departing for Egypt. From a French medieval manuscript.

After Louis' release he did not return to France, but instead sailed to Acre. He was very concerned that the cities that remained in Christian hands were poorly defended. For the next four years he concentrated on improving their fortifications. Acre, for example, had its walls and tower strengthened. However, in 1254 Louis heard that his mother had died. She had been ruling France while he was abroad. The time had come to return home.

But Louis was not finished with crusading. In 1270 Louis and King Edward I of England organized another crusade. Edward managed to negotiate a ten-year peace treaty with the Egyptians to prevent them attacking the Holy Land. Louis went not to the Holy Land, but to Tunis. He had been mistakenly informed that a show of force might persuade the Arab leader there to convert to Christianity. During this unsuccessful campaign Louis fell victim to an epidemic sweeping through the French camp and died. His bones were brought back to France and buried at Saint Denis. Miracles are said to have been performed at the site of his tomb.

Louis IX

Louis IX of France (1214–70) was just twelve years old when he became King of France in 1226. He is most famous for his crusades in the Holy Land – soon after his death he was made a saint.

His first crusade was the Seventh Crusade in 1248 . His wife Queen Margaret went with him. Louis was taken prisoner by the Saracens in 1250, but paid a ransom and returned to France in 1254.

He launched another crusade in 1270 with Edward I of England. While on the crusade he caught the plague and died.

D
SOURCE

A painting from a French medieval manuscript showing the French victory at Mansourah. Louis is on the left wearing a crown.

E
SOURCE

The flesh on our legs dried up and our skin became covered in black spots. The flesh on the gums became gangrened and no one who fell victim to the disease could hope to recover. The surgeons had to cut away the gangrenous flesh so that people could eat. It was pitiful to hear the cries of those having their flesh cut off. It was like the cry of a woman in labor.

Joinville describes the effects of disease on the French troops after Mansourah.

3.9 The End of the Crusades

During the first half of the 13th century, the crusader states were little more than a few heavily fortified coastal towns. But the Saracens were not in a position to launch any major attacks. On Saladin's death his empire split up and none of the rulers of the individual states felt powerful enough to attack the Franks. It seemed easier to make truces with them especially as the Muslims were making money by trading with the Frankish States.

Since the Franks didn't think there was a genuine threat, they failed to keep their defences in good condition. Also there were few reinforcements from Europe. New crusaders thought it was more useful to fight for Christianity in Spain, Egypt and the Baltic. But in 1244 the Muslims recaptured Jerusalem (the Christians had captured it briefly in 1229 with Barbarossa) and inflicted a heavy defeat on the Franks at Gaza. This new threat did not stop the Franks quarreling among themselves. There were even times when they went to war with each other.

Hope came for the crusader states in 1260 when a new force entered the area. These were the Mongols from eastern Europe. The Mongols hated the Muslims, so the Franks hoped to reach an alliance with them. But in 1260 the Mongols were defeated by the Muslims of Egypt. In 1261 **Baybars** became the Sultan of Egypt and the situation became even worse for the crusader states. Baybars was a cruel and intolerant man who hated Christians. He was determined to destroy the crusader states.

By 1271 Baybars had captured Caesarea, Arsuf and Antioch. Even the mighty Krak des Cheveliers fell to his forces. When Edward of England arrived with a small force in 1271, Baybars agreed to a ten-year truce. But this did not save the crusader states. In 1289 Tripoli was captured by the Egyptians and in 1291 Acre fell after a long siege. The remaining Frankish towns of Tyre, Tortosa, Sidon and Beirut were abandoned without a fight. During the next century there were several attempts to win back the land that the First Crusade had won, but they were unsuccessful.

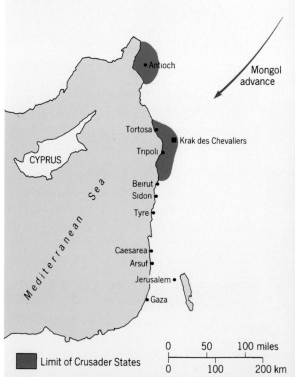

The Holy Land

- Antioch
- Mongol advance
- Tortosa
- Krak des Chevaliers
- Tripoli
- CYPRUS
- Beirut
- Sidon
- Tyre
- Mediterranean Sea
- Caesarea
- Arsuf
- Jerusalem
- Gaza

| 0 | 50 | 100 miles |
| 0 | 100 | 200 km |

◼ Limit of Crusader States

B

The fall of Tripoli in 1289. From a 14th-century Italian manuscript.

D

No one knows as well as I do of all the mean and treacherous sins committed in Acre. That is why God will have to exact such vengeance for them that Acre shall be washed clean in the blood of its inhabitants.

The Pope's representative commenting on the behavior of the citizens in Acre in 1256.

Baybars I

Baybars I (1223–77) was really called Al-Malik az-Zahir Rukn ad-Din Baybars. He was the most famous Mamluk Sultan of Egypt and Syria which he ruled from 1261–77.

He was captured and sold into slavery around the year 1242, and was bought by the Sultan of Egypt who sent him for military training. He became one of the Sultan's personal bodyguards.

Baybars fought in the Sultan's army and won several victories. In 1261 he took power from the Sultan. He made many reforms, but his main ambition, however, was to drive Christianity from the East. By the time he died, in 1277, the crusader states were nearly defeated.

C

We took the city by storm on Saturday. You would have seen your knights under our horses' hooves, your houses ransacked, your women sold four at a time and bought with your own money. You would have seen the crosses in your churches smashed and your Muslim enemy trampling on the place where you celebrate your mass, cutting the throats of monks and priests at their altars. You would have seen your palaces on fire and your dead burning in this world before going down to the fires of the next.

A letter sent by Sultan Baybars to Bohemund, Prince of Antioch, who had been in Tripoli when Antioch was attacked.

3.10 The Crusades – a Summary

The Albigensian Crusade

This crusade was launched by Pope Innocent III after preaching campaigns had failed to wipe out a **religious sect** or group called the **Cathars**, who rejected the teachings of the Catholic Church. The crusade gets its name from the French town of **Albi** – one of the main centers of Catharism.

This crusade was unusual because it was launched by Christians against fellow Christians. There were terrible massacres and much of the area around Albi was devastated. But Catharism was not wiped out.

The Children's Crusade

There were two separate children's crusades in 1212. One group came from France and the other from Germany. Many of the children on these crusades were never heard of again.

Edward I

Edward I (1239–1307) became Governor of Gascony before he was thirteen and married Eleanor of Castile when he was fifteen. He played an important part in defeating the barons who were opposing his father, King Henry II. He went on a crusade in the Holy Land where, in 1272, he heard that his father had died and he was king.

He has become famous for his use of Parliament to help him govern and for his legal reforms.

Edward I was determined to rule successfully in Britain, not just in England. His campaigns in Wales to establish his rule were highly successful. He defeated Llewelyn at Gwynedd and built a chain of castles around North Wales to ensure that there would be no more Welsh rebellions. In 1296 he invaded Scotland and took the Scottish king, John, prisoner. After this he was nicknamed 'Hammer of the Scots'. He was not as successful in Scotland as he had been in Wales, however, and the Scots eventually beat the English back.

Spain

During the 8th century the Muslims of north Africa captured almost all of what we call Spain and Portugal. Christians spent 700 years trying to recover the land. (The Spanish called this the **reconquista**.) During the 12th and 13th centuries it was common for the Christian campaigns to be granted crusader status by the Pope. By 1270 virtually all of Spain and Portugal had been recovered.

Tunisia

St Louis' Second Crusade

The Baltic Crusades

These campaigns were conducted against a group of Slav people known as the **Wends**. They lived along the shore of the Baltic and were skilled hunters and fishermen. Their religious beliefs caused great concern in western Europe. The Wends built wooden temples in which they kept effigies (statues) of their gods. More worrying, they were said to carry out human sacrifices. The German lords who carried out the crusades were more interested in taking the Wends' land than changing their religion. They didn't manage to do either.

The Holy Land

People's Crusade   *First Crusade*
Second Crusade   *Third Crusade*
Sixth Crusade   *Crusade of St Louis and Edward of England*

The Sixth Crusade was unusual in that it was led by by a man who had been excommunicated (expelled from the Church) and involved virtually no fighting. The Saracen leaders were quarreling among themelves and so Frederick II, the Holy Roman Emperor, was able to win back Jerusalem by negotiation. However by 1244 the city was again in Saracen hands and it remained so until 1917.

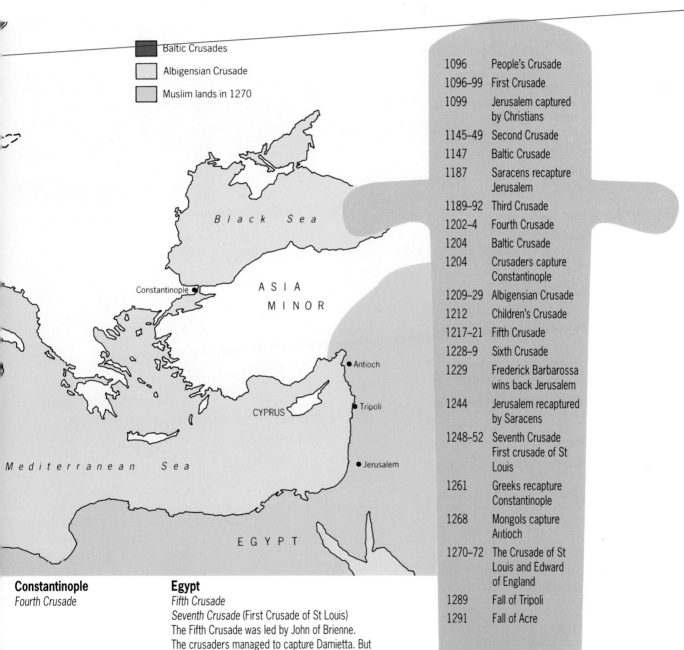

Baltic Crusades

Albigensian Crusade

Muslim lands in 1270

1096	People's Crusade
1096–99	First Crusade
1099	Jerusalem captured by Christians
1145–49	Second Crusade
1147	Baltic Crusade
1187	Saracens recapture Jerusalem
1189–92	Third Crusade
1202–4	Fourth Crusade
1204	Baltic Crusade
1204	Crusaders capture Constantinople
1209–29	Albigensian Crusade
1212	Children's Crusade
1217–21	Fifth Crusade
1228–9	Sixth Crusade
1229	Frederick Barbarossa wins back Jerusalem
1244	Jerusalem recaptured by Saracens
1248–52	Seventh Crusade First crusade of St Louis
1261	Greeks recapture Constantinople
1268	Mongols capture Antioch
1270–72	The Crusade of St Louis and Edward of England
1289	Fall of Tripoli
1291	Fall of Acre

Constantinople

Fourth Crusade

Egypt

Fifth Crusade
Seventh Crusade (First Crusade of St Louis)
The Fifth Crusade was led by John of Brienne. The crusaders managed to capture Damietta. But they could get no further and were forced to return the city before leaving Egypt.

4.1 Taking the Cross

People went on crusades for a number of reasons. Often they went for more than one reason. Perhaps the most important reason for most people was that they thought God wanted them to do it. This is a **religious reason**.

During the **First Crusade**, 40,000 people traveled to the Middle East. Of these, only about 4,500 were knights. The rest were poorer men and women. They went because they thought that good Christians should recapture Jerusalem from the Muslims. As these crusaders traveled they took part in religious services and prayers. Often they went without food for a time. This is called **fasting**. They believed that God would be pleased with them. He would then forgive them the bad things that they had done in their lives.

People made a **vow** to go on a crusade. This was a promise made to God. Once a person promised to go on a crusade the Church tried to make sure that they went. Some Church leaders even said that the promise was **hereditary**. This meant that if a parent promised to go but died, a child should go in their place.

Between 1128 and 1137 a Church leader called Bernard of Clairvaux wrote a book. It was called ***In Praise of the New Knighthood***. In this book he said that the best knights were the ones who were willing to leave home and go on crusade. These were the people that God approved of. These knights thought that Jerusalem was the holiest place on earth. They thought that they should use force to make sure that it was ruled by Christians. They wanted Christians to be able to go there without anyone stopping them. These knights, from northern Europe, were sure that God had given them the power to take and rule Jerusalem. They thought that anyone who stood in their way was an enemy of God.

The Church promised to look after the lands and property of people who went on a crusade. Often the Church would buy their land off them. This gave them the money to go. It also made the Church richer.

SOURCE A

In order to get the forgiveness for my crimes which God can give me, I am going to go on a pilgrimage to Jerusalem.

The French crusader Nivelo de Freteval, in 1096.

SOURCE B

It was the wish of King Robert the Bruce of Scotland that his heart be taken on crusade after he died.

From 'The Book of the Medieval Knight' by S. Turnbull, 1985.

St Bernard of Clairvaux

Bernard of Clairvaux (1090–1153) was one of the most important 12th century church leaders in France. In 1112 he joined the monastery of Citeaux. Life at this monastery was very strict. In 1115 Bernard was given the job of setting up a new monastery, at Clairvaux. This was very hard work and took over ten years. It was during this time that he wrote the first of the books which made him famous. Encouraged by Pope Eugenius III and the French King Louis VII, Bernard supported the Second Crusade (1147–9).

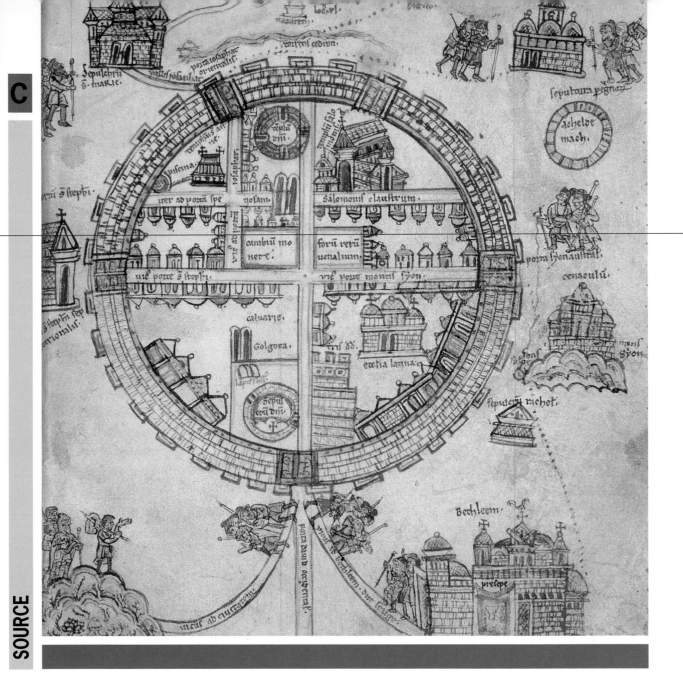

C

A 12th-century map of Jerusalem. The city is shown as being round. This is to make it look perfect and at the center of the world. Pilgrims can be seen walking along the roads towards the city. Maps like this were popular in the late 11th and early 12th centuries.

D

We urge you to do your best to defend your brothers and free the churches. We give to all those fighting on this crusade the forgiveness of sins.

Pope Calixtus II speaking to crusaders going to fight in Spain, 1123.

E

If an outsider were to hit any of your family, wouldn't you get revenge for your relative? So there's even more reason to get revenge for God. He has been thrown out of his lands, crucified.

Baldric of Bourgueil, describing Jerusalem ruled by Muslims.

4.2 Power and Wealth

In the 11th century the population of north western Europe was growing. There were many local rulers competing for power. They were violent and ready to take more power and land if they could. Some of these local rulers had originally lived in **Normandy**. These **Norman** knights had been forced to leave Normandy. So they took land elsewhere in Europe. Norman knights were in control of **Sicily** and southern **Italy** by 1091. They fought the Christian Emperor of **Byzantium**.

The Norman knights liked the idea of crusading. It gave them the chance to become more powerful and rich. They could take more land for themselves, this time in the Middle East. Many did not mind whether they took land from the Christians of the Byzantine Empire, or from the Muslims.

Other people also thought that they could become richer by supporting the crusades. The Italian cities of **Pisa**, **Genoa** and **Venice** had powerful fleets. For many years they had been trading in the eastern Mediterranean. By supporting the crusades they hoped to control more of the buying and selling in the Mediterranean. Italian ships carried crusaders to the Middle East. When the crusaders captured Acre and Tyre, the Italians used these cities as bases for their trading ships, which carried goods like spices.

A **SOURCE** The Venetians, the Genoese and the Pisans bring into Egypt the choice products of the west, especially weapons. This helps Islam and hurts Christians.

The Muslim leader Saladin.

B **SOURCE** They were attempting to seize lands and goods no longer easily available in the west and they could do this with clear consciences because their enemies were infidels [not Christian].

A view of western crusaders from 'History of the World' by J. Roberts, 1980.

The spice trade in Asia and the Middle East in the 12th century.

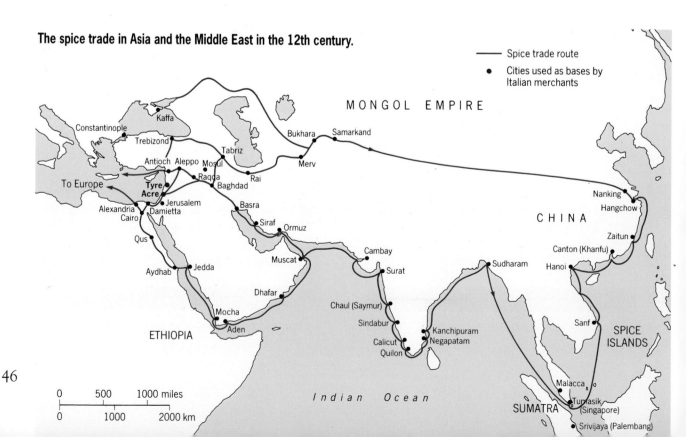

— Spice trade route
• Cities used as bases by Italian merchants

MONGOL EMPIRE

Constantinople · Kaffa · Trebizond · Bukhara · Samarkand · Tabriz · Antioch · Aleppo · Mosul · Merv · Rai · Raqqa · Baghdad · **Tyre** · **Acre** · To Europe · Jerusalem · Basra · Nanking · Hangchow · Alexandria · Damietta · Cairo · Siraf · Ormuz · CHINA · Qus · Cambay · Zaitun · Muscat · Surat · Sudharam · Canton (Khanfu) · Hanoi · Aydhab · Jedda · Dhafar · Chaul (Saymur) · Sanf · Mocha · Sindabur · Kanchipuram · Calicut · Negapatam · SPICE ISLANDS · Aden · Quilon · ETHIOPIA · Malacca · Tumasik (Singapore) · SUMATRA · Srivijaya (Palembang) · Indian Ocean

0   500   1000 miles
0   1000   2000 km

Knights were not the only people hoping to get rich in the Middle East. Many poorer people hoped to as well.

Between 1085 and 1095 there were floods and famines in many parts of northern France and western Germany. This left many people keen to start a new life somewhere else. Many of these poorer people also went on crusade. They were often led by men and women who claimed that God had told them to lead an army to Jerusalem.

Poorer people joined crusades because they were fed up with their lives. They wanted land and a chance to start again. Some of them came from the growing towns of Europe. Some came from the countryside.

Some landowners encouraged poorer people to travel to Jerusalem. They hoped to use them to farm the land. In 1120 volunteers from southern France were settled in the village of **Magna Mahumeria** (in modern Israel). Other villages were also set up in the 12th century.

The People's Crusade (1096), the **Children's Crusade** (1212) and other crusades in 1251 and 1309 were all made up of poorer people. Most of these crusaders never reached the Holy Land. Many of them attacked and robbed Jews and wealthy people in their own countries.

Peter the Hermit

Peter the Hermit (born c.1050) traveled widely in 1095, encouraging people to support the First Crusade. Starting in France and Germany he raised thousands of supporters in what became called the People's Crusade of 1096. Many of these people were poor and, by the time they reached what is now Turkey, he could not control them, so he left them. They were destroyed by Turks; he reached Jerusalem with the First Crusade, in 1099.

C

SOURCE

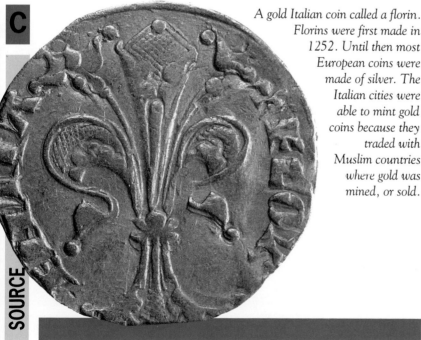

A gold Italian coin called a florin. Florins were first made in 1252. Until then most European coins were made of silver. The Italian cities were able to mint gold coins because they traded with Muslim countries where gold was mined, or sold.

4.3 Getting to Jerusalem

Going on crusade was not cheap. It could cost a knight almost five times the amount of money he gained from his lands in a year. Most people did not have this much money. Many crusaders sold some of their land to raise the cash they needed to go on crusade. Others allowed people to rent their land. Often the land was sold, or rented, to the Church.

The knight needed money to buy weapons and enough horses for the journey. He might have to pay for travel on a ship. Food would have to be bought. It all cost a lot. Poorer crusaders often walked huge distances.

Most crusaders traveled in a group. This gave them company and protection. Many went with a more powerful knight as their leader. The earliest crusaders often traveled to Constantinople. Here they met up with other crusaders before setting off into the Muslim lands. Later, many crusaders traveled directly to the Middle East by ship. English ships sailed from the ports of Southampton, Hastings, Dover, London and Ipswich. Many French and German crusaders traveled to the Italian ports of Lucca, Pisa and Genoa. From here, ships took them to the Middle East. By 1098 many of these crusaders sailed to Antioch, in modern Turkey.

SOURCE A

Some of the poorest people in the crusading army always marched barefoot, carried no weapons, had absolutely no money, but entirely filthy in their nakedness marched in advance of all the others and lived on roots of plants.

Guibert of Nogent, 1099.

SOURCE B

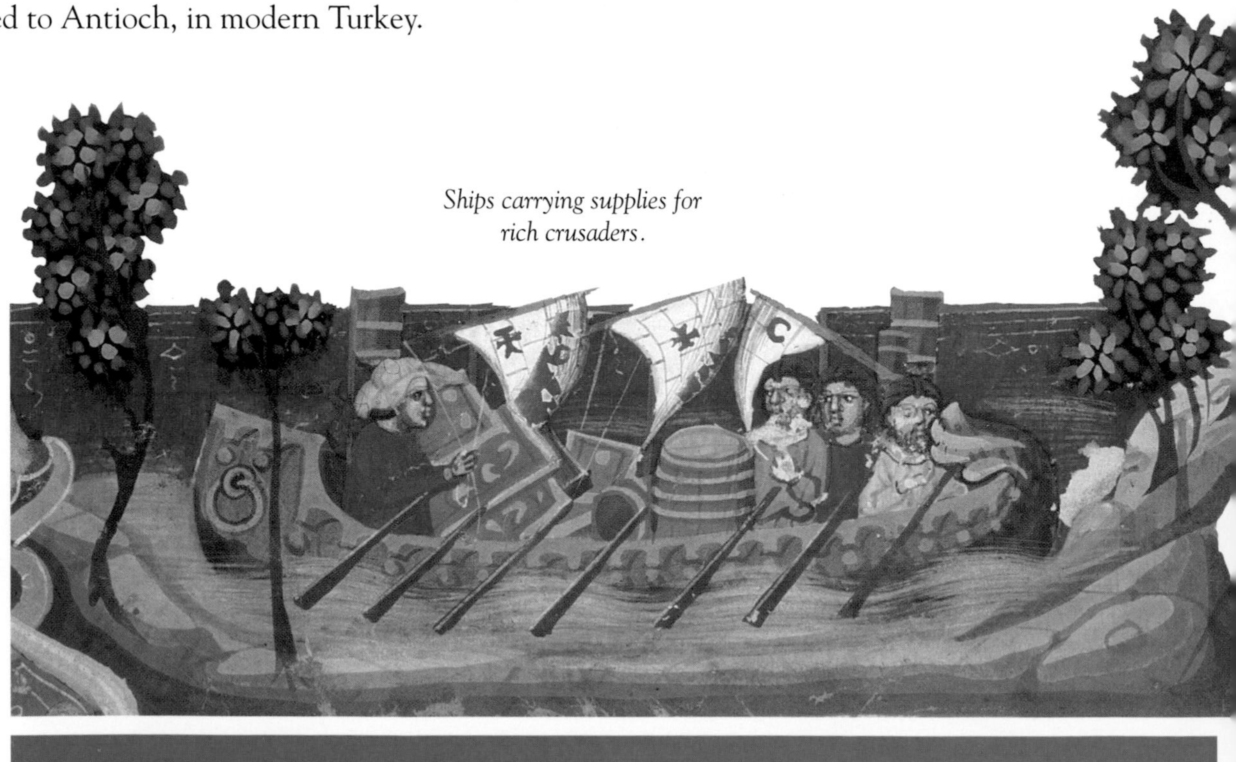

Ships carrying supplies for rich crusaders.

Traveling on a crusade was hard for all those who went. However, rich crusaders usually had enough money to pay for the things they needed for the journey. Kings who went on crusade often took money from their countries to pay for the journey. This is called a **tax**. The special tax used to pay for a crusade was called a **crusade tax**.

Many ordinary people went on the first crusades. By the time of the later crusades, in the 13th century, only wealthy knights could afford to go. Most of their soldiers were paid to go with them. They were no longer volunteers.

Poorer crusaders often ran out of money. Then they often stole to feed themselves. This made them very unpopular with the people whose lands they traveled through.

There were no real **maps** to help crusaders find their way. They usually had to pay a local person to **guide** them. It took crusaders four months to travel from Nicaea to Antioch. This was a distance of 450 miles. On this journey they lived on salted pork and biscuits. Often they could not find enough clean water to drink. On the first two crusades, more crusaders died from starvation and thirst than from fighting in battles.

Some crusaders were well-organized. King Richard of England set up a base on the island of Cyprus. From here, ships brought food to his army. He even employed a group of servants to clean and look after the clothes of his soldiers.

C **SOURCE**

In 1096 Robert, Duke of Normandy, suddenly decided to go to Jerusalem. He rented his lands to his brother William Rufus, King of England, for the sum of 10,000 marks [$7,000].

The 12th-century historian, William of Malmesbury.

D **SOURCE**

Robert, Duke of Normandy, began the journey having gathered for himself a great army of Normans, English and British. With so great a crowd traveling along the road from the west, the army became so large that one could see an uncountable crowd from many lands and languages. They were not gathered into one force until they reached Nicaea.

Fulcher of Chartres, 1096.

Gerald of Wales

Gerald of Wales (born about 1146) was born in south-west Wales. Gerald, also known as *Giraldus Cambrensis* in Latin, was a church leader and historian who defended the rights of the Welsh to run their own church, instead of the Normans.

He had been educated in Paris and when he returned to Wales, in 1175, he was made Archdeacon of Brecknock. The next year he failed to become Bishop of St Davids and returned to Paris.

In 1184 he entered the service of King Henry II of England. He visited Ireland in 1185 with Prince John and in 1188 traveled through Wales on a long journey with the Archbishop of Canterbury designed to encourage soldiers to join the Third Crusade.

Gerald wrote detailed accounts of his travels and these tales of his journeys give us valuable evidence about life in the 12th century, as well as about raising armies for the crusades.

4.4 Soldiers of God

The crusader armies who went to fight in the Middle East were made up of knights on horses, called **cavalry**, and foot soldiers, or **infantry**. The knights did most of the fighting. In a battle the knights formed three lines. The best-equipped knights were in the front line. The less well-armed knights were in the second and third lines. The job of the first line was to charge into the enemy army and fight their knights.

The foot soldiers were usually armed with **spears**. They stood close together and pointed their spears towards the enemy. This 'wall' of spears was meant to keep the enemy knights away. Men armed with **bows** and **crossbows** stood behind the soldiers with spears. They fired arrows at the enemy. After the archers had fired, the knights would charge.

Turkish soldiers fought differently. Instead of heavily-armored knights they used **fast horsemen**. They circled the crusaders at high speed and fired arrows at them. When the crusader knights attacked them, the Turks would ride away. As the knights chased them, other Turks would attack from behind. This way of fighting was new to the western knights. They did not like it and many were killed.

A painting from a 14th century manuscript showing Saladin attacking Jerusalem in 1187.

B SOURCE

The Turks are not loaded with armor like our men. When attacked by a more powerful army, they ride away on horseback. When you stop chasing them, they will attack you again. If you attack them, they will ride away once more.

A soldier in the army of King Richard of England, 1191.

C SOURCE

As the enemy soldiers have no discipline they become confused after they have charged. You can pretend to run away and then turn and catch them. You will find them totally confused.

The Byzantine Emperor Leo describing how to fight western crusaders.

A SOURCE

Turkish horsemen retreat from heavily-armored western crusader knights.

The fighting in the Middle East was different from anything western knights had experienced before. Many knights were only interested in glory and getting at their enemies. They were not used to obeying orders. They easily fell into the traps set for them by the Turkish soldiers. It was not so bad fighting **Egyptians**. They fought more like the western knights.

The crusaders soon learned their lesson. They became more disciplined. They chose places for battles where they could not be surrounded. When they marched, they did so like a **moving fortress**. The infantry marched on the outside. The knights rode protected from attack. This was very important. Otherwise the expensive warhorses, or **destriers**, could be hit by arrows.

The crusaders also learned new ways to surround, or **lay siege to**, cities and castles. During the crusades there were many sieges and few big battles. The early crusaders had few weapons capable of breaking down walls. Only rarely could they break into a city.

The descriptions of medieval battles by chroniclers and eye-witnesses are not detailed or accurate enough for the movement of troops on the battlefield to be worked out. In some cases it is not even possible to locate the battlefield itself.

From 'The Wars of the Crusades' by T. Wise, 1978.

Fulcher of Chartres

Fulcher of Chartres (born about 1059) wrote one of the most famous and reliable sources of information about the battles of the First Crusade. It is difficult for historians to find reliable primary sources on these battles, but most historians consider that Fulcher is fair in his views.

He began to work for Baldwin of Flanders in 1097. Two years later, he traveled with Baldwin to Jerusalem and spent the rest of his life there. His history of the First Crusade was written between 1101–27.

5.1 'Them' and 'Us'

The main armies fighting each other in the crusades belonged to different religions. The two greatest religions involved were **Christianity** and **Islam**. Each army believed that God was on its side. For the followers of Islam this meant Allah. For the Christians it meant Jesus Christ. This meant that each side could claim that their enemies were fighting a war against God.

For many years Christians and Muslims got along quite well in the Middle East. This changed when the first western crusaders arrived. In north western Europe there was only one religion – Christianity. The western crusaders were not used to getting along with people of a different religion. They called the Muslims **pagans** and **infidels**. They believed that the Muslims were enemies of God.

Many of the crusaders wanted to stop Christians and Muslims from becoming too friendly. In 1120 a big meeting of crusader leaders was held at the town of **Nablus**, in modern Israel. It was decided that no Christian should marry a Muslim. The meeting also said that no Muslim should wear western clothes. This was to make sure that everyone knew who was a Muslim.

In 1215 the **Bishop of Acre**, James of Vintry, complained that too many crusaders were mixing with Muslims. He wanted the two peoples to be kept apart. It was hard to make sure that this happened. Fewer western crusaders than native people lived in the lands captured during the crusades. This meant that the western crusaders were a **minority** of the population.

A **SOURCE**

For the medieval historian the world was full of rigid lines and divisions. A world divided into us and them, white and black, Catholics and pagans.

From the magazine 'Medieval World' by S. Lambert, 1991.

B **SOURCE**

The view of Islam expressed in early crusade writings was utterly negative, with the Muslims portrayed as enemies of God and servants of the devil.

From 'The Atlas of the Crusades', 1991.

C **SOURCE**

A western picture of the Muslim leader Saladin. It dates from the 14th century and makes him look like a hero.

D They painted their bodies, their faces and their chests, even their feet so that they looked like devils and demons. So that they looked like Saracens.

A 12th-century poem describes how a crusader disguised himself as a Muslim.

E There sits Orable, the African lady. She is more white than the snow in the sunshine, she is more red than the most fragrant rose.

A 12th-century poem describes a Muslim princess who helped crusaders.

G The successes of Saladin were so shocking to the Franks that they searched desperately for explanations. What they came up with was the idea that anyone so wonderful must have Frankish blood in him.

From the magazine 'Medieval World' by S. Lambert, 1991.

F

A western picture of Turks attacking Christian civilians.

El Cid

El Cid (1043–99) was really called Rodrigo Diaz de Vivar. Although he was a Christian knight, he was prepared to work with other Christians and Muslims. He was made military commander for the Christian King of Castile in 1065. In 1081 he was exiled for disobeying the king and attacking the city of Toledo. He then went on to serve the Muslim rulers of Saragossa, also in Spain.

While working for the Muslims he made plans to have his own kingdom. In 1094 he captured the Muslim city of Valencia, and ruled it until his death in 1099. Later Spanish historians and writers built up his reputation as a hero, a Robin Hood type. A 20th century Hollywood film about his life followed the lead given by these writers and presented him as a Spanish national hero.

5.2 Learning from Each Other

During the time of the crusades, Christians and Muslims met each other regularly. It was not always on the battlefield. In many places they lived in the same cities and towns. Meeting together gave them the chance to learn from each other.

Christian knights who went to live in the Middle East found the people there had a different way of life. They ate different foods. They dressed in different clothes. They knew different things. Some crusaders copied the new things that they saw. Christians and Muslims were not only living together in the Middle East. They lived together in Spain and in Sicily too. It was in these places that most of the sharing of ideas took place.

Muslim doctors were skilled in **medicine**. They used **Greek ideas** which had been lost in the west of Europe. Some used drugs which western people had never seen.

From the 12th century, the Arab way of **writing numbers** became popular in the west. These are the numbers still used in Europe today.

During the 12th century, Christians visited Spain and Sicily to learn about Arab **scientific ideas**. They **translated** books from **Arabic** into **Latin**. Latin was the language used in books in Europe. Our modern word '**chemistry**' is from the arabic word '**al-khemia**'. The word '**alcohol**' is from '**al-kohl**'.

Western builders copied some of the building styles found in the Middle East and Spain. **Pointed arches** were used in many buildings by Muslim builders. This style of building was first used in northern Europe in about 1109. This was in the building of the church at Le Wast, in France. The church was paid for by the mother of the crusader **Godfrey of Bouillon**. He was King of Jerusalem.

Not all the ideas were copied by the Europeans. Ideas were also shared. These shared ideas led to the use of **windmills, compasses, gunpowder** and **clocks**.

A  **SOURCE**

Wherever contact occurred with Islam, in the crusading lands, Sicily or Spain, western Europeans found things to admire: silk clothes, the use of perfumes, more frequent baths.

From 'History of the World' by J. Roberts, 1980.

B **SOURCE**

The Franks [in the Middle East] seem to have made no attempt to learn from native medicine. There is no record of any effort by the Franks to study local scientific knowledge.

From 'A History of the Crusades' by S. Runciman, 1954.

C **SOURCE**

Work was done by scholars who went to Spain and Sicily and collected Arabic books there. This advance of learning was not a result of the crusades and would have taken place without them.

From 'The Crusades' by T. John, 1972.

The Lion Court in the Alhambra Palace. This is in Granada, in Spain. The palace was built by Muslim builders. Some of their ideas were copied by Christians.

- sugar
- melons
- cotton
- ultramarine dye
- damask cloth.

Goods from the Middle East which became popular in Europe at the time of the crusades.

Godfrey of Bouillon

Godfrey of Bouillon (1060–1100) was Duke of Lower Lorraine and the leader of the First Crusade. After Jerusalem was captured by the crusaders in July 1099 he became king and ruled the crusader state until his death. Godfrey had many reasons for going on the crusade – religious belief, desire for adventure, failures to run his lands properly. He went with his brothers Eustace and Baldwin. When Godfrey became ruler of Jerusalem he refused to be called king, believing that only Christ was King of Jerusalem. Instead he was called 'Guardian of the Holy Sepulchre'. Godfrey defeated an Egyptian attempt to retake the city but when many crusaders returned to Europe he found the city hard to defend. He was regarded at the time as a crusader hero.

5.3 The Lessons of War

Crusaders learned many new things about fighting while they were on crusade. One of the things they learned was how to build stronger castles.

Arab and Byzantine castles were very strong and difficult to capture. They had **flanking towers** which stood out from the walls. These made it difficult for attackers to get close to the walls. The city of Antioch had 400 towers like this. The castles had platforms sticking out from the top of the walls. These were called **machicolations**. From these platforms, rocks and hot liquids could be dropped on to the heads of attackers. **Battlements** were put on top of the walls to protect soldiers defending the castle.

A

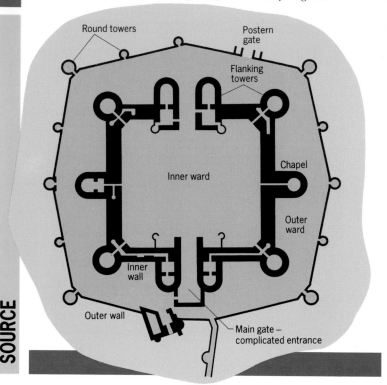

A plan of Beaumaris Castle, in North Wales. It was built between 1295 and 1323 by King Edward I of England.

B

Plan of the 13th-century castle Krak des Chevaliers in Syria.

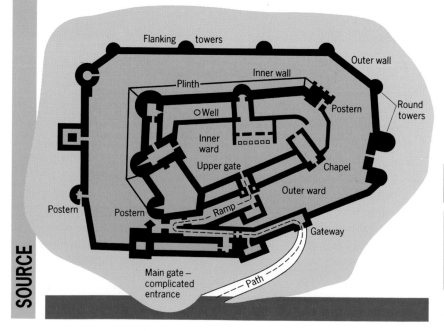

C

In the art of warfare, apart from castle building, the west showed again and again that it learned nothing from the crusades.

From 'A History of the Crusades' by S. Runciman, 1954.

A modern reconstruction of the Castle of Belvoir. The original castle was built near Lake Galilee in modern Israel. It was built shortly after 1168. It was the first ever concentric castle. This means it had walls built one inside the other.

Castles in the Middle East often had round towers. This made it impossible to dig under a corner to make it collapse. Often there was a secret gate into the castle called a **postern**. There was usually more than one wall surrounding the castle. These castles were built from stone.

During the crusades, castles were used as places where kings and rulers could live, safe from attack. From this base, the ruler controlled the local area.

Soldiers went out from the castles to fight the enemy. Between 1187 and 1189 Saladin captured 50 crusader castles. He was able to do this because the soldiers from them had come out to fight him at the **Battle of Hattin** (1187). A castle was easier to capture if it only had a few people to defend it.

Crusaders copied the castles that they found in the Middle East. Huge castles like the ones at Saone and Krak des Chevaliers, both in modern Syria, were built by the crusaders. Instead of the simple wooden castles built in Europe, these were built just like Arab and Byzantine castles.

When the crusaders went home they took the new ideas about castle building with them. King Edward I of England went on a crusade in 1270. When he came home he had his new castles built like the ones he had seen in the Middle East. Some of these can still be seen, for example in Conwy and Beaumaris, both in North Wales.

Reynald of Chatillon

Reynald of Chatillon (died 1187) was born in France and left for the Holy Land in 1147. He fought first for King Baldwin of Jerusalem and then for Constance, the ruler of the city of Antioch. She fell in love with Reynald and married him in 1153, making him Prince of Antioch.

Reynald was a brave but violent man. He was brutally cruel to a local church leader to get money from him. He became an ally of the Byzantine emperor and then betrayed him. When Constance died in 1163 her son by her first husband became ruler of Antioch and Reynald returned to Jerusalem. In 1181 he broke a peace treaty that had been agreed with the Muslims. This led to war with Saladin. Reynald again broke a truce with Saladin in 1186. He was captured at Hattin and beheaded by Saladin himself.

5.4 Trade and Influence

The crusades helped the cities of Italy to increase their wealth and power. After the capture of the crusader city of Acre in 1291, the crusaders were left in control of only the islands in the eastern Mediterranean. These included **Cyprus**, **Rhodes** and **Crete**.

From these islands it was still possible to control ships carrying goods to and from the Middle East. Christian merchants at **Famagusta**, in Cyprus, traded with the Muslim ports of **Beirut**, **Acre** and **Alexandria**.

The Pope tried to stop people from trading with the Muslims. He said that no Christian should buy and sell things in Beirut or Alexandria. This is called an **embargo**. However, this did not stop Italian merchants from trading. In 1344 the Pope realized that his embargo had failed.

Merchants from the Italian cities of **Venice** and **Genoa** settled in Cyprus and Crete. They bought spices, sugar, rich cloth and cotton from Muslim merchants. Then they sold these to people in Europe. They made a lot of money out of this trade.

Other Italian merchants from **Sicily** traded for gold with the north African city of **Tunis**. Spanish merchants, from **Aragon**, traded with **Algiers** for wool and animal skins.

SOURCE B

The most obvious result of the crusades was increased trade with the east.

From 'The Crusades' by J. Kerr, 1966.

SOURCE C

Networks of trading posts were established and continued to flourish long after the crusading kingdoms had died.

From 'Newnes Historical Atlas' by R. Moore, 1983.

SOURCE A

A modern reconstruction of a war galley from Sicily.

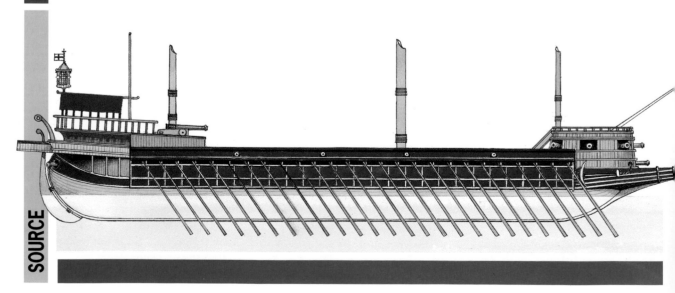

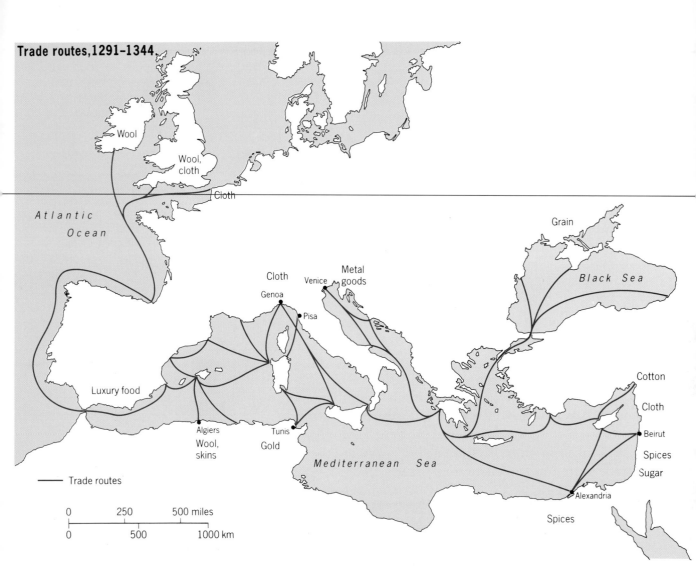

Trade routes, 1291–1344

Wool

Wool,
cloth

Cloth

*Atlantic
Ocean*

Grain

Cloth
Venice
Genoa
Pisa

Metal
goods

Black Sea

Cotton

Cloth

Luxury food

Beirut

Algiers
Wool,
skins

Tunis
Gold

Spices

Sugar

Mediterranean Sea

Alexandria

Spices

— Trade routes

0	250	500 miles
0	500	1000 km

D The trade between east and west, though it was increased by the crusades, did not depend on them for its existence.

From 'A History of the Crusades' by S. Runciman, 1954.

E Trade with the eastern end of the Mediterranean, which was already flowing before the crusades, continued and increased when they were over.

From 'The Crusades' by T. John, 1972.

Pope Clement VI

Pope Clement VI (1291–1352) became Abbot of the monasteries of Fecamp and La Chaise-Dieu and pope from 1342–52. Clement decided that his first duty as pope was to encourage a new crusade against the Turks. In 1344 he organized a crusade which captured the city of Smyrna (in Turkey) and stopped Muslim pirates using it. He could not, however, stop Christian cities from trading with the Muslims. During his time as pope he lived at Avignon in France because of trouble in Italy. He supported painters and scholars and was a wealthy ruler.

5.5 Defenders of Christendom?

When the first crusaders went to the Middle East, at the end of the 11th century, they went to defend Christians. The Christians who were threatened were members of the Byzantine Empire. Less than 110 years later, the Byzantine Empire had been wrecked. Its capital city, Constantinople, had been looted. All of this had been done by crusaders.

Many people went on crusades to get land and power for themselves. They did not care if they took it from Byzantine Christians, or from Muslims. In 1204 the **Fourth Crusade** captured the capital of the Byzantine Empire. The crusaders then took land for themselves in Greece.

The rich Italian cities were glad to see the Byzantine Empire in ruins. Now no one would compete with them for the right to trade in the Middle East. This was what mattered most to them.

Most of Greece was divided up between the Italian cities of **Venice** and **Genoa** and the King of **Sicily**. In 1261 a new Byzantine Empire was founded. This time it was very small and weak. It had to fight both the Muslim Turks and the Christian crusaders who had taken land in Greece. In 1311, Spanish soldiers in the Byzantine army revolted. They set up their own country called the **Duchy of Athens**. This caused more trouble for the Byzantine Empire.

The last eleven emperors of Byzantium fought hard to survive. They could not do so. In 1326 they lost more land to the Turks. In 1453 the Byzantine capital, Constantinople, was captured by the Turks.

The crusader kingdoms in Greece and on the Greek islands eventually fell to the Turks.

B SOURCE

Better to see in the city [Constantinople] the power of the Turks than that of the Pope.

A Byzantine official, in 1439. Like most people in the Byzantine Empire, he was a member of the Orthodox Church. Orthodox Christians did not get on well with the Catholics, led by the Pope. Almost all crusaders were Catholics.

C SOURCE

For more than two centuries Byzantium fought a losing battle for survival and not only with its Islamic neighbours. It was the west which had first reduced Byzantium to a tiny patch of territory and had sacked her capital.

From 'History of the World' by J. Roberts, 1980.

A SOURCE

The Turks have overrun the eastern [Orthodox] Christians right up to the Mediterranean sea. So if you leave them alone much longer, they will grind under their heels the faithful of God [Christians].

Pope Urban II, speaking at Clermont in 1095.

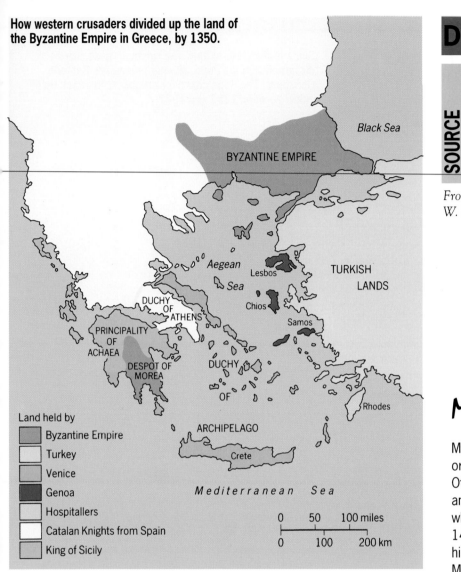

How western crusaders divided up the land of the Byzantine Empire in Greece, by 1350.

Black Sea

BYZANTINE EMPIRE

Aegean

Lesbos

Sea

TURKISH LANDS

DUCHY OF ATHENS

Chios

PRINCIPALITY OF ACHAEA

Samos

DESPOT OF MOREA

DUCHY OF

Rhodes

ARCHIPELAGO

Crete

Mediterranean Sea

Land held by
- Byzantine Empire
- Turkey
- Venice
- Genoa
- Hospitallers
- Catalan Knights from Spain
- King of Sicily

0	50	100 miles
0	100	200 km

D SOURCE

The Latin Christians insisted on trying to force the Orthodox Christians to accept their version of Christian beliefs. The Muslims were prepared to let Christians follow their own beliefs.

From 'A World History' by W. McNeill, 1979.

The kingdoms in Greece had been captured by 1456. The Genoese kept the island of **Chios** until 1566. The island of **Rhodes** was captured by the Turks in 1522. The island of **Cyprus** was captured by the Turks in 1571. The Venetians kept **Crete** until 1669.

The Byzantine Empire had stood in the way of the powerful Muslim states. The western crusaders had destroyed it. With the empire gone, the other Christian kingdoms were eventually captured one by one.

Some historians say that the crusaders slowed down the advance of the Turks. Others say that by destroying Byzantium, they got rid of the only Christian state which could hold back the Turks.

Mehemet II

Mehemet II (1432–81) was ruler, or Sultan, of the Turkish Ottoman Empire from 1444–6 and 1451–81. It was Mehemet who captured Constantinople in 1453. He became sultan when his father, Murad II, resigned. Murad then changed his mind, but Mehemet became sultan again when Murad died.

Mehemet tightened his control over the army and made peace treaties with Christian Venice and Hungary so they would not help Constantinople to resist him. Using huge cannons he captured the city. He gave himself the title 'Kayser-i-Rum' (Roman Caesar). His empire grew; he attacked Italy in 1480, but did not gain lands there.

5.6 Crusades after 'the Crusades'

Many books end their study of the crusades at the end of the 13th century. This is because this was when the last crusader kingdom at **Acre** was destroyed. The crusades that many people are most interested in are the ones which aimed at capturing Jerusalem from the Muslims. By 1300 this type of crusade had failed.

The success of the **First Crusade** made people at the time think that it was possible for Christian crusaders to control the Middle East. Two hundred years later it was clear that this was not actually possible.

However, this was not the end of the crusades. Other types of crusade continued. Some of these had been going on for some time. Others were very different from the wars to capture Jerusalem.

The crusades against the Muslims in **Spain** continued. In 1492, the last Muslim kingdom in Spain, **Granada**, was defeated. Crusades also continued on the shores of the **Baltic**. Many crusaders traveled there from all over Europe. In **Lithuania**, they fought people who were not Christian.

Some of the cities in Italy. The rulers of these cities disagreed with the Pope, although they were Catholic Christians. The Pope called for crusaders to attack these cities, between 1303 and 1387.

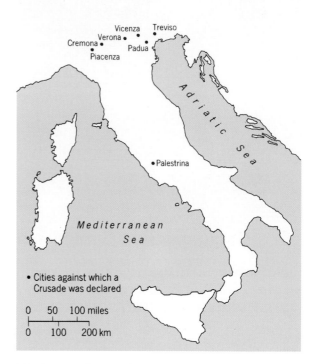

The fortress of Marienburg, in modern Poland. In 1309 the German crusaders, the Teutonic knights, set up their headquarters here. They fought the non-Christian Lithuanians.

B

SOURCE

A Christian soldier in war-torn Lebanon in the 1990s. Many Christians survived when the Muslims captured Lebanon in the 13th century. For centuries they remained independent. They look back to the crusader kingdoms as the best time in their history. Today there is still warfare between Christians and Muslims in the Lebanon.

In the 1320s and 1360s the Pope called for crusaders to attack the city of **Milan** in Italy. This was because the rulers of the city had argued with the Pope.

Between 1378 and 1417 there were two **rival popes**. One was in **Rome** and the other in **Avignon**, in France. They both called for crusaders to attack the other one.

In **Bohemia**, in modern Czechoslovakia, there were people who thought that the Pope was running the Church badly. They were called **Hussites**. Between 1420 and 1436 the Pope called for crusaders to attack them. There were five crusades against the Hussites. Despite this, the Hussites survived.

There were also other crusades against the Muslims in the Middle East. These were no longer aimed at capturing Jerusalem. Instead, these crusades tried to stop the Turks from becoming more powerful. In 1456 a crusade stopped the Turks from capturing Hungary. In 1571 a fleet of crusader ships defeated the Turkish fleet at the **Battle of Lepanto**. In 1588 the Spanish Armada attacked England. King Philip of Spain treated this campaign like a crusade.

These later crusades were very different from the early ones. For a start, they had nothing to do with Jerusalem. More than this, they showed that the Christian countries of western Europe could not unite against an enemy. This had been difficult in the 12th century. By the 16th century it was impossible.

C

SOURCE

We are weighed down with war between France and England. But when they have made peace, I shall do my best to gather a Catholic army to destroy the Bohemians [Hussites].

The Catholic Cardinal Henry Beaufort, 1427.

Henry Beaufort

Henry Beaufort (1374–1447) became Chancellor of England in 1403 and Bishop of Winchester in 1404. He fell out with King Henry IV's friends but became more powerful when Henry V and Henry VI ruled England. He became a cardinal in 1426 and tried to organize peace between England and France in 1435 and 1439 but failed. In 1443 he retired from politics.